Extreme Sports *Kris Wood*
Of
The Maritimes

Lobster Suppers, Fire Hall Bingo,
Flea Markets, Church Chowder
and
All the Rest

Pat Wilson
and
Kris Wood

Pottersfield Press, Lawrencetown Beach, Nova Scotia, Canada

National Library of Canada Cataloguing in Publication Data

Wilson Pat
Extreme sports of the Maritimes: Lobster suppers, fire hall bingo, flea markets, church chowder and all the rest / Pat Wilson and Kris Wood

ISBN 1-895900-55-7

1. Amusements − Maritime Provinces − Guidebooks
2. Maritime Provinces − Guidebooks
I. Wood, Kris   II. Title
FC2024.W54 2003   917.1504'4   C2003-901739-7
F1035.8.W54 2003

Cover design: Dalhousie Graphics

Pottersfield Press acknowledges the support of the Canada Council for the Arts which last year invested $20.3 million in writing and publishing throughout Canada. We also acknowledge the financial support of the Government of Canada through the Book Publishing Industry Development Program for our publishing activities. We also acknowledge the support of the Nova Scotia Department of Culture and Tourism, Cultural Affairs Division.

Pottersfield Press
83 Leslie Road
East Lawrencetown
Nova Scotia, Canada, B2Z 1P8
Website: www.pottersfieldpress.com
To order, phone 1-800-NIMBUS9 (1-800-646-2879)
Printed in Canada

 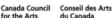 

Contents

For Gladys Westhaver
Who taught us all we know.
Love and thanks,
Kris and Pat

Preface

There are those whose idea of extreme sports includes sky-diving, bungee jumping, Australian rules football, white water kayaking, and motocross racing.

This book is not for them.

There are others who jog five miles every morning, have a lifetime membership at the gym and play on old-timers hockey teams.

This book is not for them, either.

For those people who play eighteen holes of golf every Saturday, regularly show up on the tennis courts, and swim laps at the local pool . . . ditto.

This book is written for those who, like us, don't like anything (well, almost anything), that makes them sweat. Like us, they believe that "golf is a good walk spoiled" (to quote Mark Twain), and the only good thing about cold water is adding it to Scotch whisky. If they should feel an urge to exercise, they lie down until it goes away.

When people ask, "So, what do you do for excitement in the Maritimes?" we're never lost for an answer. Our extreme sports give us just as much heart-pounding, pulse-throbbing, adrenaline-rushing, endorphin-releasing excitement as any maniac will ever experience going over Niagara Falls in a barrel. The sports jock beach boy who finally manages to "hang ten" on the perfect 20-foot wave has nothing on us.

If you've been looking for excitement in all the wrong places, if your get-up-and-go has got-up-and went, if your spirit is willing but your knees are shot, if you'd like to "just do it" but not right now, then you've come to the right book.

From the thrill of yelling "Bingo" in the Jackpot Game to the discovery of untold treasures at the flea market, to the mountain-top elation of finding actual pieces of real lobster in the festival chowder, to the boldness of penetrating the *terra incognita* of a fabled casino, it's all here.

For the top twelve extreme Maritime sports, you'll find:

a. Information on how the sport is played;

b. Tests to determine whether this is the right sport for you;

c. Tools, tips and techniques to make it more enjoyable for you;

d. Personal testimonies of those who have played the sport;

e. Skill building exercises and insider secrets.

Whether you read the guide cover to cover, or just sample a little bit here and there, you'll find all you need to join the elite ranks of the top Maritimes sporters.

Love
Pat and Kris

P.S. Don't forget your first aid kit and plenty of liniment!

The Bingo Game –
An Extremely Serious Sport

Serious:
a. requiring much thought or work,
b. of or relating to a matter of importance,
c. not joking or trifling; being in earnest.

At any time, on any day, in any community, in any place in the Maritimes, you'll find The Bingo in full swing. The Bingo is more than just a game of chance. It's an opportunity to catch up on the news, exchange knitting patterns, meet old friends and introduce Cousin Jane from Ontario to everyone else in the community. It's a little outing for Uncle George who lives in the nursing home, a night on the town for young mothers, a place where four generations can get together and enjoy a common sport. From twelve to ninety-five, they're all welcome.

Although The Bingo is fun, it is a serious business for some people. These are the folks who arrive with their good luck charms and a belief that tonight's jackpot belongs to them, whether it's a thousand dollars, a box of groceries or twenty pounds of lobster.

The Sport

1. Playing Field: Minimum requirements are a small community hall, one washroom (coed), no ventilation, a collection of miscellaneous rickety chairs and folding tables (prone to fold at any moment), plus a sound system that cannot distinguish between B and G or 50 and 60. Usually adorned with hand-lettered signs like "We do not take post-dated cheques for bingo." May have a concession booth offering stewed tea, syrupy coffee, powdered milk, assorted soft drinks, chocolate bars, and chips which run out long before the intermission so that the booth closes almost immediately after it opens. Parking is usually a muddy field next door, but it is free.

2. Players: Anyone with more than $10 to blow on an evening's entertainment. This is an individual sport; however, small teams may be formed when two or three players decide to go "sharesies" on their winnings.

3. Equipment: Hall/caller/bingo ball machine, plus some method of recording the called numbers (either an electronic board or hand-lettered cards on hooks). Players require purchased cards and personal "daubers" (pronounced "dobbers," see the glossary at the end of this chapter).

4. Object of the Game: To get a "bingo."

> Years ago it was customary to play bingo at baby and bridal showers. All the women in the community went to every shower whether related to the girl or not. Even if you didn't know the girl's name you still went. For an hour or so you played bingo, usually before they opened the gifts, made a hat out of a tin pie plate with all the bows from the gifts and served lunch. Every one played, and they had little prizes, like soap bars and knitted dish cloths, and such. The cards were on boards, most of them pretty beat up with being played so often, and you covered the numbers with counters or corn kernels. Heaven help you if you jostled the table when your neighbour was set to yell "Bingo."

The Bingo is getting better all the time. Kris and I both agree on that.

For one thing, it's smoke-free. No more antihistamines, mentholated hankies, eye drops or filter masks in The Bingo Bag. It's *pure* bingo – kind of like sex without a condom.

This also means we don't have to listen to the smoker two rows over who begins with a little throat clearing about the third game in, and then builds up to a crescendo of coughs, wheezes, hacks, gurgles, and retchings by the end of the evening. We always think they should bring in junior high students to listen as part of the anti-smoking campaign.

For another thing, they now serve sugar-free drinks. This means we can have diet pop at the intermission, along with our usual candy bars and chips.

And our local bingo hall has installed television monitors. No more trying to decipher whether it's a G or a B or a 50 or a 60, or if we're playing on the "orringe" or the "ol've" coloured card.

Best of all, we've finally figured out how to play. After only four years of intense training, concentrated study and dedicated teaching by Coach Gladys, we can hold our own with anyone in the hall.

Such a pity, too, since we're now banned from The Bingo. Well, not actually "banned," but certainly "muffled." Or as Archie Bunker would say, "stifled." And it's all because we had no idea how serious The Bingo is. Foolishly, we think it's just a game – fun, an evening out, a good time – that sort of thing. We always conduct ourselves accordingly.

We laugh when it's funny. Cheer when we win. Lament loudly when we lose. We chat with those on either side of us, whether we know them or not. We frequently ask Gladys what number was just called. We squabble over our snacks, bicker over the "right" dauber colour, and play with our lucky charms (Kris's jumping duckie and my whooping Bingo paddle).

We get equally excited when we, or someone else, is "set." We complain if our number isn't called and are always asking which game we're on now.

Although we have a lot of fun, it seems that this kind of "fun" isn't what The Bingo is all about.

"I heard on the grapevine," Gladys says with a lowered tone and worried expression her face, "that *they* have complained about you fellas."

We're just at the table, gathering our cards.

"Just give us whatever she gets," I say to the bingo clerk. "Only give Kris one less of everything because she's bingo-challenged."

"I am not!" exclaims Kris. "I just don't want to give up my amateur status."

"Oh right! Like the time you left me to daub your card because you had to go to the bathroom."

"Well, stop whining, Gladys did most of it."

We both burst into loud guffaws.

"Shhhh!" says Gladys urgently, looking around with wild eyes. "This is what they're complaining about."

"What??" we both say together.

"You fellas are noisy! And you're not serious enough. And you're distracting everybody else." Gladys's face flushes bright red. She's not good at being the bearer of bad news.

"Oh. That." We both scan the faces around us, looking for the finks who turned us in.

"Tough," I say. "Tell them to sit on the other side of the room."

"We're here for fun," says Kris. "And we never complained about them when we had to go home and strip buck naked in the laundry room and throw our clothes in the tub, and then have a shower before we could even get a cup of tea, all because *they* smoked like chimneys all evening long and we smelled like one at the end of it."

"Shhhh!" says Gladys. "They'll hear."

"Well, let them. I, for one, come to The Bingo for a good time, and that's what we're going to have. Right, Kris?"

"Right."

Gladys pales.

"You don't have to sit with us. We'll understand," I tell Gladys.

"No, that's all right. I'm tarred with the same brush already. Just try to keep it down a little." Gladys sits down and begins to arrange her cards.

"Are you guys going to be good this week?" someone calls over from several tables over. One of the finks, no doubt.

"We'll try," says Gladys, smiling placatingly back at her.

"No, we won't," says Kris. "This is the fun table. Them as doesn't want to have fun can sit someplace else."

And that's where it stands. The Bingo is getting better, but we're not. At least behaviour-wise.

> "Sport inevitably creates deadness of feeling. No one could take pleasure in it who was sensitive to suffering; and therefore, its pursuit by women is much more to be regretted than its pursuit by men, because women pursue much more violently and recklessly what they pursue at all." – Ouida (Marie Louise de la Ramée 1839-1908)

I worked for a time in a senior's residence. They had Bingo one night a week. It was one of the most popular activities. People would come down as much as two hours before the game started to grab their "lucky" card, and their "lucky" seat. Even if they never won a game they still believed in those special cards and seats.

Are You Up For It?

Rank the following statements on a scale of 1 to 5

1 – only to save a loved one's life
2 – as an alternative to root canal
3 – if you pay me
4 – if there's food
5 – in a heartbeat

1. It's snowing heavily. The snow plow hasn't been by. Your car doesn't have snow tires. The Bingo hasn't been cancelled. Would you go to The Bingo? _____

2. Your son is getting married on Saturday morning. The Wedding Rehearsal ends at 7 p.m. Friday. The Bingo starts at 8 p.m. Would you go to The Bingo? _____

3. You have a temperature of 101°. Your throat is sore and your head aches. Your neighbour calls and says her car won't go and she needs a ride to The Bingo. She offers to buy your cards for you in exchange for a lift. Would you go to The Bingo? _____

4. You're flying to Toronto tomorrow morning on the 6:35 a.m. flight for a work-related conference. You live two hours from the airport. The Bingo ends at 11 p.m. Would you go to The Bingo? _____

5. It's a hot summer Sunday afternoon. It's a perfect day for a picnic on the beach. Would you go to The Bingo? _____

6. Your girlfriends have planned a trip to the city to see The Chippendales Male Dancers. It's on your Bingo night. Would you go to The Bingo? _____

7. You finally get an appointment for "the works" at the Golden Dawn Spa. They're running late, and you're midway through major waxing. The Bingo starts in half an hour. Would you go to The Bingo? _____

8. Your neighbour is hosting a Chocolate Lovers Party with lots of free samples. You love chocolate. It's on same night as The Bingo. Would you go to The Bingo? _____

9. Your partner has farmed the kids out to Grandma's, opened a bottle of wine and has that look in his eyes. Would you go to The Bingo? _____

10. You know that if you leave the funeral home by 7:30, you can make it to The Bingo after Great Uncle George's wake. Would you go to The Bingo? _____

Scoring

10–19 *points*:

Obviously, The Bingo is not your sport – yet. Could it be that you have never played? Studies show that those who decry The Bingo have never been there. We suggest you bite the bullet, give it a whirl, and make sure that your apathy is due to true dislike of the sport and not to ignorance.

20–29:

You've probably tried The Bingo and are not yet a true convert. Perhaps your lack of success has turned you against the sport. It's important for you to realize that it's not the winning, but the being there, that counts. Try to relax a little and enjoy the ambiance and the company next time you get dragged along.

30–39:

You may be at that stage of the sport where a cookie jar, bonanza or jackpot will turn the tide of your feelings. Your responses that The Bingo is only an option if you're paid or fed indicates you've missed the whole point of The Bingo. You're trying too hard to be a winner and need to loosen up. Perhaps a fluorescent dauber will get you in the mood to have fun.

40-50:

We've met people like you. For you, life *is* The Bingo. You're not alone, as The Bingo halls on a beautiful Sunday afternoon in summer will attest. You, like the rest of your bingo buddies, know that the elusive jackpot/cookie jar combination awaits you someday.

> "I'm fairly confident that if I die tomorrow, Don would find a way to preserve me until the season was over and he had time for a nice funeral." – Dorothy Shula (wife of Don Shula, coach of the Miami Dolphins football team)

The Top Daubers' Essential Accessory: The Bingo Bag

No true dauber would be caught dead at The Bingo without his/her bag. Carrying one puts you into that elite class of Top Daubers. You won't find Bingo Bags in Wal-Mart, Zellers or The Bay. You won't even find them at Frenchy's or Value Village.

The Bingo Bag is a personal creation, a true expression of personality and taste.

If you go to the major bingo halls, such as some of those run by First Nations people or attached to the large casinos, you'll find Bingo Shops. Here, the bags are bingo-themed with cards, numbers, letters and daubers.

What goes in your Bingo Bag? The daubers go into the slots around the outside of the bag. You'll always need several daubers in case one colour turns out to be unlucky!

Inside the bag:
- Kleenex (for tears of joy or sorrow),
- Cello tape (more about that later),
- Candies (to contribute to the general pool with your bingo-mates),
- Gum (to relieve tension),
- Money (did we mention you have to pay to play The Bingo?),
- Lucky charms (these can run the gamut from rabbits' feet to pieces of jewellry to pictures of loved ones to beanie babies),
- Personal items: glasses, antihistamines, lip gel, aspirin, comb, lipstick, etc.

Now you're ready to go to The Bingo.

The Number One Characteristic Of True Top Daubers

They never yell "Bingo!"

This doesn't mean that they don't win. They do, but they do it in a low-key, laid-back, serious manner. They say "bingo" in a conversational voice. True Top Daubers simply say "...go." No yelling, screaming, hugging or jumping up and down. (Unlike most game shows and other sports). This is important to know. Other bingo players look down upon "Bingo!" yellers – they already know they didn't win so they don't need it to be rubbed in.

If someone wins big money, the rest of the players clap. Not too loudly. They're not that thrilled.

Skill Building Exercises

The challenge of The Bingo is trying to do four things at once:

1. Listen to the caller –

Not as easy it as sounds: local accents, speech impediments, bad sound systems and general mumbling make this a real challenge for the tyro. In the more progressive bingo halls, television monitors provide a visual of the ball being called; however, this distracts your eyes from your cards, and since you can see the number before the caller announces it, there is the danger of committing the ultimate sin: calling "Bingo" before the number is officially announced.

> *It was only my second time at a bingo game, and I was really nervous. You see, half of me really wanted to win. The other half didn't because supposing I called "Bingo" and then I'd daubed a wrong number or something. I was on tenterhooks all evening. It was during the blackout game, and you could feel the tension rising as the numbers mounted on the board. All eyes, including mine, were glued on the television monitors. Suddenly, I was set! I could feel my heart pounding and sure enough, the next number on the monitor was mine. I daubed it and called "Bingo."*
>
> *A great sigh went around the room as everyone realized that they weren't going to win the blackout jackpot, and I could hear the rustling of the newsprint cards being balled up and put into the trash bags at each table. People started gathering up their things and scraping back their chairs, preparing to leave. Suddenly, the fellow checking my numbers said, "Wrong Bingo!"*

> *I just wanted to die. You see, I'd said "Bingo" when I saw the number on the monitor. The caller hadn't called it out yet, so it wasn't official. What an embarrassment as everyone sat back down, got out their cards, and re-started the game. I did win when my number was then called, but so did four other people, so the jackpot wasn't worth the humiliation I felt.*

2. Look at the card –

This is relatively easy if you play one card with three games on it. However, there is pressure to keep up with the Top Daubers, and you might find yourself faced with nine games, or even twelve games. At this point, the daubing is seldom any fun. Chess with a Russian would be easier.

3. Daub a number if called –

Again, this is relatively easy for the Top Daubers because they know which numbers are under what letters. For the rest of us, if we miss the letter, (see number 1 above), we futilely search for the number 60 under the letter I. Many of the bingo callers tend to stress the number, not the letter, so, to the untrained ear, they all sound the same.

4. Constantly monitor for the winning pattern –

This is hell. Generally speaking, the beginner can either daub or monitor. Not both. It's a good idea to sit with Top Daubers. Promise them half your winnings if they'll tell you when you're set, or if you have a bingo. Part of the problem is that the winning pattern changes. Just as you've figured out what two lines and four corners look like, they announce "postage stamp" or "blackout" or "inside/outside square." Like we said, it's hell.

Back to skill building. As you can see, the skills are multiple and high level. Basically, anything you do that requires you to think, look, listen and use your hands simultaneously (such as changing the baby's diaper while you watch your toddler pouring a glass of milk and listening to your 8-year-old recite the nine times table while you think about what to have for supper) will build your bingo skills.

And they wonder why more women than men play bingo.

> "Men forget everything; women remember everything. That's why men need instant replays in sports. They've already forgotten what happened." – commedienne Rita Rudner

Glossary of Terms

Dauber: An essential tool. It's a tube of liquid with a large round sponge tip. This is used to stamp a number when it's called. Daubers come in all colours. The flurorescents and the glitters are the latest on The Bingo scene. Some Top Daubers stick with one colour. Others use a different dauber for each game.

Card: These are thin sheets of newspaper with games printed on them – usually three games per sheet/card. The sheets come in a pad, each with a different colour so you know which game is being played. Some single sheets hold the specialty games. You can buy as many cards as you wish.

Game: A card(s) of one colour. The colour will be announced (whether you understand what colour is announced is purely a matter of luck).

Cookie Jar: The first number called at The Bingo. This number is now a "lucky" number, and if you win a bingo with that number, you're entitled to the Cookie Jar pot. The pot is the total of monies collected from the players who want to be included in the Cookie Jar. Your card is stamped to indicate you are a Cookie Jar player.

Jackpot: The first half of the Jackpot game is called before the regular bingo begins. The object is to get a blackout (all numbers daubed), in 54 numbers or less. So far, we've never seen it happen. The second half is called towards the end of the evening. You can buy extra jackpot cards at the intermission if your first sheet isn't looking promising. The Jackpot changes depending on how much is won each week.

Bonanza: A blackout game at the end of the regular games. It's usually worth a little more than the regular games.

Set: You only need one more number to win. In our experience, announcing to your neighbours that you are "set" guarantees that the needed number will never be called in your lifetime.

Postage Stamp: If you divide your bingo card in four, the "N" line down and the middle line across are FREE. You need to fill in the rest of the four corners – the postage stamps – in order to win.

Inside/outside Square: Often played as part of the Bonanza Game, this means that you have two other chances of winning. Inside square is all the numbers around the FREE one in the middle. Outside square is all the numbers around the outer edge of the game.

Line: Horizontal, vertical or diagonal row of numbers. Many games have combinations of lines and corners.

Four Corners: Just what it says. The four corners of the card – 2 "Bs" and 2 "Os." Regular games are usually one line and four corners to win, or two lines to win.

FREE: On all games, it's the middle number.

"Sports should always be fun." – Charles Mann, National Football League linebacker

Instant Replay

The Bingo is the extreme sport for you if you:

1. Aren't too intellectual to handle the difficulty of the bingo game.

2. Like heart-pounding, adrenaline-filled moments when you're "set," interspersed by whole evenings of ho-hum.

3. Have snobby guests you don't want to encourage to make a return visit.

Degree Of Difficulty For This Sport

A piece of cake – laughable, really, a child under four years old could play this.

☺☺ If I can do it, you can do it – a child over four years old could play this.

☺☺ Anyone can do it – you have to pay attention some of the time.

Brain cells are used – you have to think some of the time.

Don't try this at home – experienced sporters only.

How To Find This Sport

Listen to the conversation behind you in the grocery lineup (not the 10-items-or-less aisle). "Well, I was set six times last night at The Bingo. My number never came up once. Next Tuesday, I'm going to try the Lions Club. They got better cards there."

The Tourist Route Ididerod – An Extremely Popular Sport

Popular:
a. *of or relating to the general public,*
b. *suitable to the majority,*
c. *easy to understand,*
d. *commonly liked or approved.*

Fleur-de-lis Trail, Marconi Trail, Ceilidh Trail, Sunrise Trail, Glooscap Trail, Evangeline Trail, Cabot Trail, Marine Drive, Lighthouse Route, Miramichi River Route, The River Valley Scenic Drive, The Appalachian Range Route, The Fundy Coastal Drive, The Acadian Coastal Drive, Sunsets and Seascapes, Ship to Shore, Anne's Land, Charlotte's Shore, Bays and Dunes, Hills and Harbours, whale watching, bird watching, seal watching, osprey watching, tuna fishing, covered bridges, lupine looking, colour looking, historical sites, marshes, waterfalls, gorges, chutes, trails, tidal bores, reversing falls, magnetic hills, Green Gables, markets, lighthouses, boat building, historical re-enactments, nature centres, eco centres, marine centres, beaches, fossil hunting, theme parks, national parks, provincial parks, amusement parks, water parks, Cows ice cream, Ganong Chocolates, wineries, cheese factories, buskers, bald eagles and beaver tails ....

Here in the Maritimes, we know how to pull them in.

The Sport

1. Playing Field: Anywhere in the Maritimes with a road and something to look at.

2. Players: Anybody with a car, or able to get on a bus or walk/cycle/hike. Can be played individually, in small groups, or in packs.

3. Equipment: Cash, cheque book and credit cards. (Guidebook optional)

4. Rules: Two simple rules: stick to the beaten path and buy a souvenir at each stop.

5. Object of the Game: To "do" as much of the Maritimes as possible in the shortest possible time. Extra points are given when one Tourist Route is used to travel to another Tourist Route. The Pro Tourist on the Circuit can and will cover all three provinces in one week.

Five Universal Truths, Ten Mistaken Myths And Ten Good Excuses To Use The Tourist Route

Say the words "Tourist Route" to travellers and you're going to get a lot of different reactions, from appalled shock ("My dear, we never go on the beaten path.") to enthusiastic approval ("It's the only way to be sure you can find a motel or a gas station.") to lukewarm acceptance ("It's probably the quickest and simplest way to 'do' an area and get your money's worth out of the trip.").

My friend Millicent always goes the tourist route. She buys the guidebooks, gets the maps, studies up beforehand and is prepared for every day's adventures. When she knew she was coming to Cape Breton, she decided she wanted to "do" the Cabot Trail, so she refreshed her memory of high school history lessons by picking up some books at the library for winter reading. By the time she hit the Trail, she *knew as much about the area as the tour guides. She was all set to look at the historical sites, visit the churches, eat the hodge-podge (a kind of veggie soup) and rappie pie (a kind of potatoey-omelette thing). As far she was concerned, a Tourist Route was the only way to go. (Her daughter just wanted to go antiquing — she got to eat hodge-podge and rappie pie instead.)*

Five Universal Truths

1. The weather doesn't determine the success of your trip. Rain or shine, there's always something to do and see, and even if the fog rolls in, you can always watch a weaving demonstration or tour a fort.

All my life I've dreamed of going to Green Gables. I read every Anne book at least ten times when I was a young girl. Standing in front of the house was one of the most moving experiences I've ever had. Everybody laughs at me when I tell them that, but if they knew how profoundly Anne and her life affected my life, they'd understand.

2. The Tourist Routes are designed so that you get the most bang for your buck, view-wise, food-wise and interest-wise.

3. All necessities of life are always available on the Tourist Route. There are restaurants, gas stations, public restrooms, picnic areas, hotels, motels, cabins, grocery stores, snack bars, and chip wagons.

We just missed the ferry to Prince Edward Island. It leaves from Caribou, a fairly remote area with nothing but a ferry terminal and some fishing boats. But, there was a restaurant, and we had the best fish and chips ever! Thank God for ferry terminals.

4. The roads always go somewhere. They may not be the best roads in the province but they are guaranteed to take you to something worth seeing or doing.

5. They provide an opportunity to meet fellow travellers and local residents. Everywhere you go, you'll find people just like yourself, and other people anxious to make your trip enjoyable.

> *It was my birthday. We were staying at a local country inn. That night at supper, my husband asked the proprietor for some kind of birthday cake. Not only was there a cake, but the entire kitchen staff, fellow guests and a group of local diners all joined in. We had a wonderful evening.*

Ten Mistaken Myths

1. Every proprietor on a Tourist Route has one objective: to get your money.

Actually, this is true, but not in the sense of gouging or rip-off or cheating. If you have an establishment open for business, the object is to make money. Come to that, every proprietor everywhere has one objective: to get your money.

2. You don't see the "really good stuff" on a Tourist Route.

It depends upon what you call the "really good stuff." If you want to see yards full of broken down cars and old fridges, or the local dump, or a swamp or two, then by all means, get off the Tourist Route. If you want to see views of the ocean, historic sites and tourist attractions, then the Tourist Route is the best way to do so.

3. The Tourist Route is phony – the country/province isn't really like that.

Thank God. None of us could keep up the "quaintness" required for those living along many of the Tourist Routes. The rest of us live quietly out of sight, looking and acting just like the people you left back home.

4. You pay extra for everything on the Tourist Route.

Not true. You'll pay more for a motel room in one little town that has no other choices than you will in a city full of motels. Ditto for gas. And if you've ever bought a loaf of bread in the far reaches of a Maritime province, you'll know it's a lot more expensive than in a major centre.

5. Everything is crowded.

O.K., if you must go on the Canada Day weekend to the Number One Tourist Attraction in the province, it will be crowded. But then, so will the recreation spots back in your home town. Travelling on the shoulder seasons – spring and fall – means that you'll often have the Tourist Route to yourself.

6. Everything is made in Japan, Korea or Taiwan.

Not. Many souvenir shops are very particular about their merchandise and have a policy of selling only "local" and "indigenous" goods. Having said that, look at the label. If it says "Taiwan," complain and don't buy it. The proprietor will eventually get the message.

7. Nothing measures up to the glowing advertisements on television.

If you've ever bought a Thigh Buster or an SUV or a thing that slices as it dices as it cuts as it chops, this will not be news to you. Why should tourism be any different?

8. You won't find any surprises on the Tourist Route.

Believe us, a burst tire is about all the serendipity most people can handle on a trip.

9. You'll have to compete with bus tours to see or do anything.

Here's a little known secret: look in the parking lot. If there's a bus there disgorging passengers, go have lunch elsewhere.

10. Everything is completely organized and you have no freedom.

It's like television. There are hundreds of channels, organized to the second, but you can choose anyone you want. That's freedom.

If you do a Tourist Route out of season, be warned. The major attractions and views will be there but the service stops may not. We did the Lighthouse Route last November. It was a fabulous day, with bright sun, fall colours and even the occasional lighthouse, but the necessities of life had vanished with the tourists. No bake shops, no antique stores, and no ice cream parlours eased our way. Worst of all there were no gas stations either and not only were we travelling in the glow of the low gas warning light, but I really needed to find a bathroom. So be warned. Take the Tourist Route any time, but take sandwiches and a thermos as well as a spare gas can, and make sure you go before you leave home.

Ten Good Things You Know About The Tourist Route

1. You know where you're going and how long it will take you to get there.

2. You know you'll find a place to stay and something to eat.

3. You know you won't be stranded far from a gas station or help.

4. You know you can always go shopping if the weather is bad.

5. You know there will be things for the kids to do.

6. You know there aren't long, boring stretches of highway driving.

7. You know you'll see the best views and sites of the area.

8. You know you'll be able to get souvenirs and postcards (and a lobster trap, or two).

9. You know everyone on the Tourist Route is there to help make your holiday great.

10. You know you'll have bragging rights when you get home because you went somewhere recognizable.

The Tourist Route is Travel 101 in any province. Once you've done it, you're ready to branch out on your own and go exploring the highways and byways, dirt roads and cart tracks, loops and dead ends that take you to some of the unknown areas "far from the madding crowd."

> There are three types of football players. First, there are those who are winners and know they are winners. Then there are the losers who know they are losers. Then there are those who aren't winners but don't know it. They're the ones for me. They never quit trying. They're the soul of our game. – Bear Bryant, U.S. college football coach

Dennis and Inez, friends of ours from Toronto, drop in with their trailer on their way to Newfoundland. "We've heard so much about Nova Scotia," gushes Inez, "and we're just dying to see everything. We've put aside a whole day for it."

"A whole day?" I say incredulously.

"Well, it does seem a lot of time, I know, but then, we did Europe (Yurp) in eight days."

Who can argue with logic like that?

Pat and I have a brief consultation with the *Doers and Dreamers Guide* (which we call the Gapers and Gawkers Guide), and decide that the Lighthouse Route to Peggy's Cove and Mahone Bay should just about fill the bill of "doing" Nova Scotia in a day. Fortunately, the lupins are out, so we can tell them everywhere in the Maritimes looks more or less the same. Besides, they'll never know any differently.

Pat, as always, opts for an early start, but Inez and Dennis linger over a late, late breakfast and it's 10:30 and several returns for vital articles (camera, camcorder, sweater, hats, sunglasses, water bottles, gummy rubbers, rain coats, umbrella, cookies, sun block, and cell phone) before we finally hit the road. "Thank God we're not doing Africa in three days," Pat mutters *sotta voce* to me.

We whiz straight through to Halifax, and after one of our usual near-death experiences on the Armdale Rotary, we turn off to Peggy's Cove.

"Ohh, look," screams Inez. "A yard sale! Let's stop."

Twenty minutes and a plastic lighthouse ("Perfect for Aunt Sophie, and look, it really lights up.") later, we're ready to roll. Unfortunately, Dennis has disappeared. We find him across the street talking to a homeowner about the concrete gnome in his yard.

"We can pick up one of these just down the road," he says enthusiastically. "There's a place that makes them, and we can just keep it in our trailer until we get home."

"I don't remember seeing a gnomery in the *Doers and Dreamers Guide*," Pat mutters. She's doing a lot of muttering. She's definitely not Tourist Route material.

We stop at the garden centre, and after much discussion, a gnome joins us on the trek. We're fifteen kilometres away from Halifax.

"Are we there yet?" asks Inez. "I'm very hungry and you said there was a restaurant at Peggy's Cove."

"About half an hour," I say soothingly.

"If we keep driving without any more stops," Pat mutters.

"Oh, look!" It's Inez. "There's a cute little tea shop just up the road, and it's got a gift shop, too."

"Oh goody," mutters Pat.

"There's coffee and scones," I tell her. "And cream, and jam, and cake, and you can buy some homemade bread for Gerald."

"I'm not buying him anything," Pat says fiercely under her breath. "He was supposed to come with us. I'm sure he and John could have fixed your pump some other day."

The tea shop is twee beyond belief. Fishing nets, clam shells, glass floats, plastic starfish and big hunks of cork adorn the walls. Anything that can be is tole painted with jolly sailboats, lighthouses, sea gulls, whales, dolphins and mermaids.

"It's wonderful," cries Inez, panning across the room with the camcorder.

Dennis is already in the gift shop. Before we've ordered chowder and biscuits, he's back with three large painted rocks, one with the *Bluenose*, one with a lighthouse and one with a seagull. "For the guys at work," he says. "We'll just put them in the trailer until we get home."

Pat and I settle down into our bowls of chowder. Inez and Dennis are flitting about the room, picking up and putting down items, ooohing and aaahing over tole painted things and happily piling up a stack of purchases on the counter.

We finally pull them away an hour later.

"Did they eat at all?" I ask Pat.

"Who knows? They sure bought a lot." She hands me a biscuit. "Here's Dennis's biscuit. Put it away. We may need it before this trip is through."

"Where are they?" I ask, putting the biscuit into the glove compartment. "Their stuff is here, but I don't see them."

We hear Inez's voice. "Oh, look. An antique store."

Sure enough, across the street, the siren call of an antique store has lured them in. We trudge over in their wake. Inside, the basement of a regular suburban house is now home to a miscellaneous collection of "antiques".

"I hate this sort of place," I tell Pat. "I can remember using most of this stuff. Does that make me an antique, too?"

Pat isn't listening. She's sitting morosely in a rocking chair. "We'll never get to Peggy's Cove at this rate," she mutters.

Dennis is now in deep discussion with the proprietor. "Guess what," he says. "There's a guy down the road who collects model boats and he sells them, too. We could get some for the grandkids. We'll put them in the trailer until we get home."

Ten minutes later, we're knee-deep in model boats in some guy's garage. Dennis buys two and adds them to the pile in the back of the van.

"Are we there yet?" asks Inez.

"Just another twenty minutes," I say.

"As long as we keep driving," Pat mutters.

By now we're into Peggy's Cove country. Miles of barren black rocks, scree, bogs and boulders.

"Stop the car," says Dennis. "I've got to get pictures of this."

He's out like a shot, and scampers over the nearest boulders and disappears from sight.

We wait patiently for ten minutes.

"Pass me the biscuit," says Pat.

"I'm going to get him," says Inez. "He can't have gone far."

"Oh no you don't," says Pat. "I'll find him."

Eventually, we're back on the road. It's now late afternoon.

"Oh look," says Inez.

"Oh, no," says Pat.

On the left is a huge gift shop called Jennifer's of Nova Scotia that screams "buy me, buy me." My heart sinks. The car park is jammed. This is obviously a hot spot for tourists. We pull in between an SUV from Vermont and a Cadillac from Texas.

"I'll wait here," says Pat, settling down for a snooze.

Inside, the place is jammed to the rafters with every possible Maritime craft – weaving, pottery, pewter, woodwork and jewellry. Dennis and Inez are lost in seconds. I wander around in a desultory sort of way, and eventually go back to the van to join Pat.

"Where are Dennis and Inez?" she asks, sitting up.

"They're still in there," I say.

"It's nearly five o'clock. It'll be dark before we ever get to Peggy's Cove and we might as well forget about Mahone Bay."

"Never mind," I say soothingly. "They're having fun."

By 5:30, we're back on the road. It's easy driving since most of the traffic is now leaving the area.

"At least we'll find a parking spot," says Pat.

"Near the store," suggests Inez. "I've heard they have a fantastic gift shop there."

"You might like to look at the lighthouse," I suggest.

"Oh, do they have stuff for sale there?" Inez asks.

"Well, you can buy postcards and have them cancelled with the Peggy's Cove stamp," I tell her.

In the lighthouse, Inez settles in happily to write a postcard to every person in her address book. Dennis and his camera disappear around the corner.

"Does he know not to tread on the black rocks because they're slippery when they're wet?" I ask Pat worriedly.

"Who cares?" Pat mutters. "Let's go find something to eat."

We agree to meet them in the restaurant. The restaurant at Peggy's Cove is cunningly designed so that you can't enter it except through the souvenir shop.

"We're doomed," says Pat, pressing past yellow oilskin hats and T-shirts and bins full of polished rocks. "We'll never get them out of here alive."

We're well into our third cup of tea before Inez and Dennis join us. "We just put our shopping bags in the van," she says, "and I've sent everybody a postcard so they'll all know we've been to Nova Scotia."

Eventually, we manage to tear them away only to have to stop at Beale's Bailiwick in the village. They disappear inside.

"I didn't get to see the stone wall carvings," I complain. "It's the only thing I really like here."

"Stop whining," says Pat, "or I'll send you in there after them."

By now it's beginning to cloud over and the sky is dark.

"We'd better head back," I say. "It's a good two hours to home."

"Oh, but I wanted to see the Swissair Memorial," says Dennis. He slips another roll of film in his camera.

"O.K., but it'll have to be quick." We load up their latest purchases and head off down the road.

The Memorial is awesome, sitting under lowering skies, with a light fog drifting in from the ocean. Just a few rays of setting sun light up the area. The big boulders stand like sentinels, and I hope that this will bring Dennis and Inez some perspective on the real Nova Scotia.

Dennis is obviously impressed. We leave him to snap away happily.

Inez stands in the middle of the Memorial.

"It's very nice," she says. "But I think they really ought to have a souvenir shop. You know, with little rocks and things...."

Instant Replay

The Tourist Route is the extreme sport for you if you:

1. Like things organized and nailed down.

2. Want to see a lot of different things in the shortest possible time.

3. Like to travel in a pack.

Degree Of Difficulty For This Sport

☺☺ A piece of cake – laughable, really, a child under four years old could play this.

If I can do it, you can do it – a child over four years old could play this.

Anyone can do it – you have to pay attention some of the time.

Brain cells are used – you have to think some of the time.

Don't try this at home – experienced sporters only.

How To Find This Sport

Follow the big bus marked "Talkaboutit Maritime Tours."

The Craft Show Junket —
An Extremely Festive Sport

Festive:
a. relating to a period or program of cultural events or entertainment.

The concept of 3 full days, 12 hours a day, 250 vendors, unlimited opportunities to snack plus the bonus of free parking, all for the price of an admission ticket that is good for the whole period of the show, might seem like a little bit of heaven.

For real buyers, it is. They come to a craft show to buy things. They appreciate the vast gamut of crafts on display, and have a real sense of the skills and time needed to produce these items. They're the reason crafters continue to exhibit in craft shows.

However, the vast majority of people who come to the craft show aren't buyers and don't buy. They have a different agenda for the craft show:

- An opportunity to take Great Aunt Emily out of the nursing home for an outing. While they're at it, they'll bring along the kids, strollers and all.

- An opportunity to see all the latest craft ideas and get ideas for their own crafting efforts. (Note: these are the folks who pepper the vendor with questions such as "How many coats of paint do you put on that? Did you get the pattern out of a book? Where can I buy those ribbons?")

- An opportunity for a girls' day out. Lunch at the community food concession, fudge from the booth by the door, and a couple of drinks in the beer garden, and the day is a success. Crafts? What crafts?

- An opportunity for professional browsers to practice their browsing skills. Every item is examined, held, commented upon, and returned to its place before moving on to the next item.

- An opportunity for group homes, nursing homes, seniors tesidences, convalescent facilities and schools to bring a group of their charges for a field trip.

- An opportunity for desperate hosts to get their guests out of the house on a rainy day.

The craft show is planned to appeal to all groups. From the initial decisions by the show committee on who is invited to exhibit, to the size of booth, to the number of participants, to the price of a ticket, to the hours and length of the show, everything is geared towards entertainment of one sort or another.

The Sport

1. Playing Field: Large space (convention hall, arena, curling rink, fair grounds) that can be divided into innumerable smaller areas. Ample free parking (with the exception of the city venues which offer metred street parking or indoor parkades). Food concessions are mandatory.

2. Players: Two teams: Buyers and Sellers.

3. Rules: Buyer: you must pick up as many objects as possible and give every indication that you are planning to buy the object without actually buying it.

Seller: you must keep the buyer at your booth until the only way the buyer can escape is to purchase something from you.

You may use guilt, coercion, flattery, price adjustment, rudeness, pretentiousness, tears, entreaties, humour, and fear to achieve this end.

4. Object of the game: Buyer – buy as little as possible. Seller – sell as much as possible.

"We're in!" I wave the wad of papers jubilantly. I'm not surprised. I knew that our stuff would past muster for the prestigious Lunenburg Craft Festival.

"So, what do we have to do?" Kris asks.

I shuffle through the pile. "OK. They don't supply anything. That means we'll need to rustle up tables and chairs and stuff. I've got umpteen yards of beige material I bought eons ago. We can use that for our display." I read on. "Uh oh."

"What's wrong?"

"They don't supply partitions or curtains, either. We'll have to start from scratch."

"We'll get John and Gerald to help us," Kris says. I envision multi-level shelving units and eye-catching light fixtures.

"Uh oh."

"Now what?"

"The booth is ten feet long...."

"Wow! That's bigger than our last show space."

"Yeah, but it's only six feet deep."

"Oh."

"Uh oh."

"What!"

"They suggest we bring a fan. That means they know it's going to be hot."

"We can do that."

"And a fire extinguisher."

"How hot are they expecting it to get, for heaven's sakes." The elation of being accepted into the exclusive fold of the festival is beginning to fade.

Thus begins our foray into big-time craft festivals.

Just before 8 a.m. on the first day of the festival, we jockey for space in a parking lot full of vans, trucks, trailers and RVs. Most have fancy lettering on the sides – Poppy's Closet, Kit Kat

Krafts, Leather Luxuries, Potluck Pots. Already, we're beginning to feel a little intimidated by what is obviously a crowd of veterans of the craft show junket.

At 8 a.m., precisely, the doors are thrown open. We're carried in on a tide of people into a huge, empty arena, with numbered spaces carefully chalked out on the concrete floor. I wonder how they decide who goes where. Before we can even find our number, the booths are half erected. Sounds of hammers, drills, saws and curses fill the air. We join right in.

"Funny, this went together fine at home," I say, trying to shove one piece of Styrofoam into its designated slot.

"At least it's light," Kris reminds me. "I'm glad that we opted for thick Styrofoam over plywood." She looks smugly at our neighbour who is struggling to erect her pegboard walls.

We'd already scouted out the location of the nearest Tim Hortons the night before. It's strategically placed between the motel and the arena. At nine, we send Gerald out for coffee and donuts.

At ten, we send Gerald to find a lumberyard. We need wood. Stryofoam may work for shelves, but it doesn't do the job on our trestle table.

By the time he returns at eleven, we need coffee again. Gerald volunteers to go. "The car's right at the door already," he says. "It's easier than trying to find a parking space."

By twelve, it's looking good. The arena is now a marketplace. It becomes obvious that the committee had thought this out carefully. No one is next door to a competitor – not easy with more than two hundred booths.

"Lunchtime," I announce.

"Tim Hortons?" Kris suggests.

"Where else?"

We're back at one for the official opening of the show. "It'll probably be pretty light to start with," says Kris. "Like our other shows."

"People say this one's well attended," I tell her. "Perhaps we'll be busy."

"Don't cry for me, Argentina…." I'm humming along with the music from a large theatre organ set up near the door, being energetically played by a fellow in a shirt and tie – an anomaly in the casually dressed crowd.

We don't look up until several hours later. We haven't sold a huge amount, but if the oohings and ahhhings are any indication, we're in the market.

I decide to go and find tea. I'd seen on the information sheets that there is a special room set aside for the vendors. There I meet several other vendors and it's obvious this is a close-knit cadre of regulars who "do" shows from one end of the Maritimes to the other. The talk is of which shows are "good," and which ones bombed. No one talks of their personal sales. This seems to be a taboo subject. I bring back tea for Kris.

"Midnight...not a sound from the pavement...," Kris is singing enthusiastically. "The organist is obviously an Andrew Lloyd Webber fan," she says, doing a mock pirouette in the aisle.

"At least he's not as bad as that show we did in November. Remember we had that really depressing drippy Christmas music and then the high school band with everlasting 'Jingle Bells'?"

The crowds thin out over the supper hour. We get a chance to meet some of our neighbouring vendors. The St. George's Church Fundraisers are on one side. An incredibly busy lady photographer is on the other. As we watch her photos of Maritime flora taken on black backgrounds fly off her table, we consider a change of career.

"They may be 'artistic,' but to me, there are strong overtones of Elvis on black velvet in there," Kris whispers.

"You're just jealous because she's selling more than us."

"Am not."

Across the way, we meet a German lady with fabulous paintings on silk, a French fellow with his wife's tole-paintings, and the owner of a booth selling one-million-and-one leather belts.

Several people have asked about the small folding stools which we've brought for our own comfort. "Maybe we should get into a stool franchise," I tell Kris.

By nine, we're beat. One down and two to go.

"Let's just rearrange some stuff," Kris suggests. "We can do it now, ready for tomorrow."

We start to pull things off the shelves. The lights go out. A disembodied voice over the loudspeaker tells us to vacate the premises. We grope around in the dark, trying to throw sheets over our display, and finally give up and head out.

Saturday is hot and even busier. The day starts off well. A woman rushes back home and brings us several boxes of supplies for our craft; a boy with zingy green braces on his teeth buys three items for his family; several people ask for our business card.

"*If I were a rich man.… Ya da da da da da dahhhh.*" The music moves on to wider selection of Broadway favourites. I'm in good voice this morning.

The heat builds, but fortunately we're located in front of the double loading dock doors which stand wide open. The hamburger concession is right outside, and the tantalizing odour of frying onions wafts in on every breeze. The strawberry shortcake people by the door are doing a gangbuster business. Food is all around us.

"As they say in the real estate business, it's location, location, location," says Kris, coming back with a large helping of shortcake.

On our brief forays around the site, we find some old friends from previous craft shows: the vest people and the lady with the breathtaking stained glass, the fellow who does wooden lamps and pictures frames, and the painted tray artisan – they are all there. It's a little like a "carny family." Everyone is a craft show warrior with a story to tell.

"*Is this the little girl I carried…?*" "Fiddler on the Roof" is back for the fifth time today. We notice that the organist is doing a brisk business selling his tapes and CDs.

By four o'clock, we're getting bored. We've heard all the tunes at least twice; we've told sixteen people, "No, we don't have a pattern"; we've eaten everything in sight; we're hot and sticky; and our feet hurt.

"Have you noticed that there are a lot of really big people today?" I say to Kris. Another 300-pound fellow rumbles by. "I'm counting fat ladies. It helps to pass the time. I'm up to seven already. No, wait, make that eight."

"What about me?" she asks, looking down at her rumpled T-shirt.

"No, you're not fat enough. I mean, *really* fat ladies."

"That's not politically correct," she tells me sternly, "and not nice, either. Oh wait. There's one. Nine."

Fortunately, a customer interrupts and we lose count.

At closing, we're ready for lights-out. We're already sheeted when the buzzer sounds. We leave, humming, "*How are things in Glocca Mora…*"

Sunday is even hotter. We start our day with a pancake breakfast at the Presbyterian Church. The doors of the festival open at 10:00 and by 10:30, the place is hopping.

"Don't cry for me Argentinahhhh...." It's wearing a little thin – the same old tunes are beginning to blend one into another.

"If he does 'Phantom of the Opera' one more time, I'm out of here. I know he's good, but I can't stand it," says Kris.

"A little crabby are we?" I ask. "Too much sugar for breakfast?"

The crowd today is less intense, more ready for a day's outing and a Sunday stroll. Business is slow in the morning, but picks up by the afternoon. We're beginning to count down until closing at five. We notice thunderclouds gathering and wonder how it will bode for packing up the van.

In the vendors' lounge, the general consensus is that this hasn't been as good as other years. "Maybe the craft show business is on the way out," says the purveyor of hand-made soaps. "I think I'm going to try some U.S. shows."

"Too much hassle at the border," say another. "I tried it once. Never again."

"Oh, well, there's always the Forum Show at Christmas."

I bring back tea for Kris.

"Hello young lovers wherever you are..." The beat goes on.

"She sold my picture." Kris stops humming and hisses at me.

"What picture?"

"The heron picture. The German lady just sold it."

"But you weren't going to buy it. You haven't made enough money to buy it."

"Well, there's still an hour to go."

The last hour winds down slowly. Even the organist has switched to a tape recording. Although the contract states NO ONE IS TO PACK UP BEFORE CLOSING, we notice a lot of booths are being surreptitiously dismantled. The booth behind us is down to a table and several items. We pretend not to notice when the walls disappear.

Finally, it's over. We're packed up and out of there in under an hour. If we thought the ingress was rushed, it has nothing on the exodus. Only dust motes remain by six o'clock.

"I got plenty of nothing...," Kris sings as we pile into the van.

"Oh shut up," I say. She got that right.

"My biggest concern during a race is getting bored. The biggest thing I have to combat is falling asleep while going around and around." – Mario Andretti, race car driver.

Beware of the craft show held in winter in an arena. I did one once. Never again! The whole floor, cleverly hidden under a tarpaulin, is ice. It's cold. A damp penetrating cold that seeps into your bones. Despite being cold, it melts. Your display sags and teeters as the floor shifts beneath you. People trip over wrinkles in the tarp and careen into your artistically arranged pottery shelves, or plunk onto your stacks of prettily wrapped snowball cookies. The crowds of spectators schlepping around produce a depressing dragging sound as their sneakers scuff against the damp canvas. It drowns out the merry repetitions of "Jingle Bells," and makes a body want to go and yell, "Bah Humbug!" at the Organizing Committee.

Survivor – The Craft Show

You are the Chairperson of The Big Craft Festival in your community. Your job is to make the tough decisions to ensure that everyone who attends and participates has a good time.

You have 389 applications for booth space. The booth applications are as follows:

- 151 booths of tole-painted Christmas decorations
- 2 of fossil jewellry
- 16 of pewter ornaments
- 25 of stained glass ornaments
- 12 of dried flower arrangements
- 30 of children's wooden toys
- 29 of pine furniture
- 6 of leather crafts
- 69 of knitting/sewing/tatting doilies
- 50 of food items

You have the youth orchestra from the junior high school anxious to perform, as well as the Sweet Adelines, Charles and

Pat Wilson & Kris Wood

his Magnificent Organ, the Boggy Hollow Blue Grass Band, and the local Drum Corps.

Lining up for an opportunity to give a live demonstration are a fellow who makes wrought iron boot scrapers, your cousin Mary known for exquisite quilled greeting cards, a weaver complete with a 16-foot loom, a "live" artist who will do portraits on the spot, and the man who makes huge garden swings out of old tires.

Entertainers on the roster include Miss Pringle's ballet class, a cooking show host, the Tai Kwan Do group and the Dog Obedience School.

Your cup runneth over!

Food suggestions are coming in hot and heavy. Aside from the standard beaver tails, popcorn and candy floss, you can choose from the Hospital Auxiliary Thousand Pie Table, the Girl Guides Cookie Stall, the Firemen's Wienie Roast, The Lions' Bar-B-Q Chicken pit, the Masons' Chowder Lunch, the Women's Missionary Society Tea-Tent, and the Sea Cadets hamburger stand. Just remember: before you make any rash decisions, you have to live here.

The schedule of the show is also up to you. Three days are allotted – a Friday, Saturday and Sunday. Keeping in mind the goal of the show – people buying tickets to get in – set up a schedule to achieve this. Note: federally mandated conditions of labour do not apply to The Craft Show. A 14-hour shift is perfectly reasonable.

Finally, you need to determine how the booths will be set up. The aim is to achieve maximum density in minimum space.

Now you're ready to play *Survivor – The Craft Show.*

The object of the game: to be the last sane person left on the committee when The Craft Show is over. Bonus points are given if you can put on a successful show without being drafted again next year. Regardless of attendance figures, record or otherwise, you lose if you're asked to be chairperson of next year's committee.

"People are needed, but nobody is necessary." – Paul Brown, football coach.

Ten Things You Should Never Do When Browsing At A Craft Festival Booth

1. Never discuss your personal family matters with your friend while looking at the merchandise. It spoils the mood.

> *I overheard a woman saying to her friend as they wandered past the booth, "After his sister dies, that's the end. I'm never speaking to any of them again. They can all go to hell as far as I'm concerned." That stopped me for the next hour. Which sister? Who? And why not? I couldn't leave the booth to follow them, and now I'll never know.*

2. Never tell the craftsperson that you make exactly the same kind of thing, but yours is much better, smaller, larger, costlier, prettier, and you sell them for twice as much and export them to sixteen foreign countries.

3. Never ask the crafters for explicit instructions on how to make their crafts. Assume that they have spent many years perfecting the methods, and may not wish to make them public. Similarily, don't ask for patterns, recipes, suppliers or suggestions for instruction books.

> *The label says: ""Every item is unique; no two alike." The browser picks up and puts down several items, and then asks us if she can have a pattern. I point out that there are no patterns. That's why they're unique. "Oh," she says. "Can you draw me a picture then?"*

4. Never ask a crafter, "Why don't you have a store?" They've sold four things in the last three days, and they don't need any reminders that they can't afford to run a shop. If they have store, they'll tell you.

5. Never let your kids go off on their own. Uncontrolled children are a nightmare for the booth holder.

6. Never ask for a personal demonstration of the craft item unless you're seriously planning to buy. And don't ask for special colours etc., unless you're serious.

> *She wanted the item, but she wanted it with the decoration on another item. Did we have such a thing? I went back to the van, rummaged through six huge hampers, and finally found one. She never came back."*

7. Never eat tantalizing food in front of the crafter unless you plan to share. Many crafters are sole booth proprietors and are "trapped" there for the entire length of the show. They bring water bottles and sandwiches, and grab a quick bathroom break during a lull. These crafters are always hungry. Don't tempt them.

8. Never make disparaging remarks about the items in front of the crafter. You wouldn't allow your children to talk about his big nose in front of him, so why should you talk about the merit of his artistic attempts.

9. Never compare this crafter's items with another crafter's items. "Oh, I can get it cheaper at a booth on the next aisle." or, "I saw those for five bucks at the flea market."

10. Never talk your friend out of making a purchase. If she wants to buy it, let her.

> *The father and his younger daughter had agreed that this was the perfect gift for Mom. The teenage daughter slouched up to the booth, glanced around briefly, curled her lip and said, "Why do you want to buy crap like that?" The sale never happened.*

Instant Replay

The Craft Show is the extreme sport for you if you:

1. Like window-shopping.

2. Aren't sure what hobby you'd like to take up next.

3. Have guests and don't know what to do with them.

Degree Of Difficulty For This Sport

☺☺ A piece of cake – laughable, really, a child under four years old could play this.

If I can do it, you can do it – a child over four years old could play this.

Anyone can do it – you have to pay attention some of the time.

Brain cells are used – you have to think some of the time.

Don't try this at home – experienced sporters only.

How To Find This Sport

Admire someone's plastic canvas purse or hand-carved wood-pecker pin and ask where she got them.

The Lobster Supper Trials —
An Extremely Formidable Sport

Formidable:
a. having qualities that discourage approach or attack,
b. tending to inspire awe or wonder.

Summertime in the Maritimes means lobster for the tourists, and for the rest of us, too, if we're lucky. Churches, firehalls, community centres, school groups, and just about any organization that wants to make a buck, hosts a lobster supper. Now, we're not talking about those 100 percent tourist attractions where the whole show is orchestrated to the nth degree, and everyone knows what to do. We mean the local lobster supper, usually held once a year in small communities along the shore.

They are catch-as-catch-can affairs. The lobsters range from humongous to measly, the salads from boring to fabulous, the rolls from home-made to "store-boughten" and the desserts from blah to bliss. You can't rely on last year's feast being repeated this year. Every dinner is a new adventure.

But, one thing remains the same: the lobster. We've often wondered what intrepid person first saw one of those things crawling around on the bottom of the ocean, caught it, brought it home, and then said, "Boy, this looks tasty. Let's boil it until it turns bright red, break open its hard shell with a hammer and eat whatever we find inside!"

I saw a real live lobster this summer. It was crawling rapidly over the sea floor under our canoe. It was sort of yellowy brown, and although I wouldn't have wanted to get too close to its claws, it looked a little too puny for eating. Anyway, he was pretty safe as the season in these parts was well past. I'm not sure how fast they grow, though. Perhaps by next spring one of the local trappers will be hauling him out of the water. Maybe we'll be trying to figure out how to get him out of his shell at the next Lobster Supper.

The Sport

1. Playing Field: Any community hall, fire hall or church basement in the Maritimes that can be quickly rearranged from the bingo game the night before. Note: must have a kitchen, although hot water, dishwasher, double/triple sinks, and room to swing a lobster are optional.

2. Players: Anyone with an appetite and a sense of adventure. Again, this is an individual sport, although players may work with a more experienced partner. Pro Lobster Crackers often give free demonstrations.

3. Equipment: See Tools and Techniques.

4. Rules: There are no rules. Anything goes as long as it gets you inside the thing.

5. Object of the game: To remove the lobster from its shell without your requiring bandaids, stitches or a blood transfusion.

We have to buy tickets for the second serving: the 4-5 p.m. time slot is already filled. This is not good news. It means used salads, dry buns and picked-over desserts, which is why the 4-5 time slot sells out quickly. To add to the challenge, I'm bringing along my three grandchildren, my daughter and my mother. With Pat and Gerald, and my husband, John, we're quite a crowd. All in all, it doesn't bode well.

We're there by ten to five, and the hall is already jammed. We're lucky to find seats together down in one corner. The harassed volunteers hastily wipe down the oilcloth, remove some miscellaneous bits of lobster shell, and tape a fresh garbage bag on the end of the table. Only two partially filled salad bowls remain. I send Pat off on a foray to neighbouring tables while I get the grandchildren strategically placed between consenting adults. I butter buns for them to keep them quiet.

The coffee and tea servers are there in seconds. I always have the coffee because you can't really tell it from the tea, and tea made in a coffee pot is revolting. As well, the tea has been stewing on the back of the stove all afternoon. I've learned to grab my coffee now and not wait until the meal is over. Often, the pots never make it back again.

Pat, a veteran forager, returns with several interesting bowls of salad, some pickles and a new basket of buns.

We pick up our flimsy plastic bibs and attempt to tie them around our necks. It's not successful, and I wish I'd brought either Scotch tape and/or plastic bags.

The lobsters start arriving, each one weighing in at about one-and-a-half pounds, resplendent in all their scarlet glory on the plates in front of us. Jesse, my 6-year-old grandson, pales. Sitting high on his pile of coats, he's eye-to-eye with the monster. Seeing them in tanks at the Superstore is one thing; facing them on your plate is another.

I explain how to pull off the legs and suck out the juice.

"It's just like a Freezy," I tell the kids encouragingly.

It becomes obvious in minutes that the kids aren't up to the challenge. Fortunately, all lobster suppers have ham plates for the allergic and faint-of-heart. I ask for ham for them and a bag for me to put their lobsters in. They'll taste just as good later in the week.

Meanwhile, Pat is muttering at the end of the table. "There's no way to get into this thing." She's got the lobster that didn't receive a few preliminary cracks in its shell. There's always one which somehow slips past the hammer/hatchet person.

"I'm ok," I say, checking the back and claws of my beast. "You're going to need a hammer to get into yours."

"You don't need no hammer," Russell, one of our local friends, tells us scornfully. He reaches across the table and pounds Pat's lobster with his massive welder's fist. The lobster is no match, and Pat begins extracting it happily.

"I don't have a pick," says John.

"Yes, you do," I say. "It's that little red plastic stick by your plate."

"This thing?" John jams it into his lobster, and it immediately breaks.

Meanwhile, Gerald has joined the kids with a plate of ham. My mother and daughter opt for ham, too.

That leaves three of us to continue the battle for the lobster meat, and six lobsters to go in the freezer.

"Oh no!" says Pat. "My pick broke, too. Now what?"

"You don't need no pick," says Russell, reaching across the table and grabbing Pat's fork. Expertly, he bends back one of the middle tines to a 45-degree angle. "There," he says. "That'll do you."

I hand him my fork, too, figuring that the cost of the fork is less than the cost of new teeth.

Silence reigns for a few minutes as we pick and chomp. The lobsters are delicious, cooked to perfection. They easily make up for the paucity of salad and pickle choices.

"Ouch!" screams Pat, and holds up a bloody thumb.

I rush off and get more napkins. I should have been prepared. Pat always feels she has to make a blood sacrifice to the lobster god. When we have lobster at home, I always have bandaids on hand.

"Ta Dah!" It's John. He's got his lobster claw out in one piece. Pat and I are never patient enough to delicately pick and poke until the whole thing slides out onto our plates. Anyway, we like the tail best and save that until last.

By now, we're elbow deep in lobster run-off, bits of shell, green gunk (which John is happily spreading on a bun), and crumbled buns. Our table has all the ambiance of the aftermath of a mediaeval feast. The little flock of volunteers swoop in and helps us restore it to a semblance of civilization.

"Keep your forks," says one, "for your desserts. They're over there on the dessert table. Go and pick out what you'd like."

"Let's go hose off first," says Pat. "I hate eating dessert with sticky hands."

The Ladies Room is busy. We wait our turn at the sink and hope the water holds out. There are no paper towels left. We head for the dessert table, wiping our arms on our shirt fronts as we go.

The desserts are guarded by a dragon lady. "Only one piece per person," she says sternly. She tries to give the kids chocolate squares, but they've got their eye on the last three pieces of pumpkin pie with whipped cream. "Hff," she sniffs. "Those are usually for adults." We ignore her. We paid full price; we're owed full meals.

When we get to the table, we realize that our Russell-modified lobster forks don't work on the desserts.

"We need new forks," says Pat.

"You don't need no new forks," says Russell, bending each one back into its original state, and wiping them down on the sleeve of his shirt.

We leave, full of ham and lobster, with six lobsters in one bag and three lobster tummies for the dog in another. We're now veterans – we'll know next time to bring our own bibs, a cushion for Jesse, a box of wipes, some bandaids, and our own tools, just in case Russell isn't there.

"Nobody goes there anymore because it's always so crowded."
– Yogi Berra, Major League Baseball catcher and manager.

Are You Up For It?

Part A: Eating Habits

1. Have you ever voluntarily eaten snails (*escargots* if in a fine French restaurant)? Yes/No

2. Have you ever voluntarily eaten frogs' legs (*grenouille* if in a fine French restaurant)? Yes/No

3. Have you ever chowed down on a plate of cods' cheeks? Yes/No

4. Have you ever chowed down on a plate of prairie oysters? Yes/No (If you don't know what these are, you've never eaten them!)

5. Do you enjoy a healthy bowl of oolican? Yes/No (If you don't know what this is, you've never eaten it!)

Part B: Skills And Aptitude

1. Using no tools other than your fingers and teeth (toes excluded), have you ever removed flashlight batteries from a bubble pack in a blackout? Yes/No

2. Are you able to remove a splinter from the thumb of a screaming, squirming child? Yes/No

3. Can you pull porcupine quills from the dog's nose without injury to yourself? Yes/No

4. Are you an expert at removing the meat from nuts in their shells? Yes/No

5. Do you always scrape out the final smear of peanut butter from the jar? Yes/No

Part C: Thinking Inside The Shell

1. You frequently improvise tools to get the job done. For example, you might use the heel of your shoe for a hammer. Yes/No

2. If it's animal, vegetable or mineral, and it's not moving, you wonder if it's edible? Yes/No

3. You've always said that you can't judge a book by its cover, especially when it comes to food. Yes/No

4. If it's worth eating, it's worth working at – artichokes, corn on the cob, and almost anything sealed in plastic wrap. Yes/No

5. You might not go bungee jumping, but you'd probably go to an ethnic restaurant. Yes/No

Scoring

7–15 Yes answers:

You're probably eating lobster as you read this.

1–7 Yes answers:

There's more to life than a Big Mac. Get out there and participate in your food.

0 Yes Answers:

Skip this chapter.

Tools And Techniques

1. *Tools:* You have two options:
a) The "official" Maritime Lobster Set.
    Consists of one lobster cracker and four lobster picks.
    Actually, it consists of a small pair of pliers and four short fondue forks.
    Not recommended.

b) Your own Lobster Set.

Consists of a conglomeration of pliers, forceps, nutcrackers, tin snips, kitchen scissors, hammer, nut picks, tooth picks, skewers, fondue forks, and your high-school geometry set. This is fine-tuned by trial and error. Personal preference and desire for hygiene also play a part.

Note: When you attend a lobster dinner, take your own tools with you since the only tool provided is a plastic pick that lasts 1.3 seconds.

I found the perfect lobster tool just by chance. We were having lobsters for supper and I knew we'd left our lobster sets at the cottage. I scrounged around the tool room and came up with a hammer and pliers, fine for breaking open the shell, but I couldn't find anything to get the meat out of the shell. It was my son who suggested the compass he had in his geometry set. We tried it, and it worked like a charm, much better than anything I've ever seen in the traditional lobster sets. It didn't break, could be easily manipulated, and most importantly, was thin enough and sharp enough to penetrate right to the end of the claws. We went out and bought three more, and they're now our "official" lobster tools.

2. Clean-Up:

a) The "classy" dinners provide you with a large plastic bib, finger bowls and plenty of napkins. The waiters come around and pick up the debris.

b) The local dinners usually provide you with a flimsy bib, one napkin, and a green plastic garbage bag taped to the end of the table. We recommend you bring a plastic raincoat (the locals prefer oilskins), a box of napkins, and a box of Handi-wipes. Really refined people wear rubber surgical gloves, although we enjoy the juice running down our forearms. It adds to the general ambiance.

Note: Never wear "good" clothes to a lobster dinner.

> "It's a little like wrestling a gorilla. You don't quit when you're tired – you quit when the gorilla is tired." – Robert Strauss, director of Swim Gym

3. General Techniques:

a) If you go to a classy restaurant, they've already done everything for you. All you have to do is daintily pick up chunks of juicy lobster with your fork and dip it in the butter pot gently bubbling over the tea light. Bor-r-ri-ng!!!

b) If you go to a local dinner, most of the lobsters have three beginning cracks – the back and the two big claws – unless of course you get the lobster the fellow who's supposed to crack it for you has missed. The rest is up to you. Armed only with the useless plastic pick and a fork, you now have to dismantle the lobster and retrieve the bits of meat. This is why we recommend you bring your own bag of tools.

c) Generally, the lobster dismantling proceeds in an orderly fashion:

> i) pull off the legs (long, skinny straw-like appendages on either side), and suck out the meat. They are not "pickable" – they only squish if you try to crack them. Think of them as a small Freezy – suck, squeeze with teeth, and suck some more. This gives you time to work up to the real job at hand.
>
> ii) Pull off the claws. Set aside for the moment.
>
> iii) Pull off the tail. Set aside.
>
> iv) Now you have the "belly" left. Some people like digging around in here. They eat the green glop – the roe – spread on bread. They suck little bits of meat off the edges. Frankly, we think this is a lot of work for little reward. We save the bellies for the dog.

v) Now for the claws. Break them into sections and work your way up to the big end. Here's where your picks come in handy. If your claw has a crack along its back, it's easy to open and enjoy the meat. If not, get out the hammer or the pliers and break the thing open.

vi) The tail is considered the delicacy. Start with the little "petals" at the end of the tail. Each one has a tasty bit of meat that you can suck out. Now it's time to open the rest of the tail. Use the scissors and cut up the underside. Then peel the edges back, and theoretically, the tail meat pops out. In practice, you'll need one of your picks.

There, wasn't that easy?

> "Perhaps the single most important element in mastering the techniques and tactics of racing is experience. But once you have the fundamentals, acquiring the experience is a matter of time." – Greg LeMond, bicycle racer

Instant Replay

The Lobster Supper is the extreme sport for you if you:

1. Like to get involved with your food and enjoy hands-on dining.

2. Like a challenge.

3. Don't mind wearing your food.

Degree Of Difficulty For This Sport

A piece of cake – laughable, really, a child under four years old could play this.

If I can do it, you can do it – a child over four years old could play this.

☺☺ Anyone can do it – you have to pay attention some of the time.

Brain cells are used – you have to think some of the time.

Don't try this at home – experienced sporters only.

How To Find This Sport

Chat with people in the emergency department at the local hospital.

The Casino Spree –
An Extremely Exciting Sport

Excite:
a. to call to activity,
b. to rouse to feeling, usually by a profound moving,
c. to arouse by appropriate stimuli.

Casinos have sprung up like mushrooms in the Maritimes. Las Vegas East is a prime destination for locals and tourists alike. Maybe it's the spin-off glitter and glitz of Harrah's or Caesar's Palace, or the lavish buffets and constant availability of food and alcohol in copious quantities, or maybe it's the feeling of the so-phisticated, jet-setting high-life of Monte Carlo, or the cocooned retreat from the harsh realities of office politics, baby diapers and bunions. Or maybe it's the dream of winning a million at the slot machine.

We went because we thought it might be exciting.

Caveat: We're not talking about roulette, blackjack, craps, poker or other serious games of chance. This is about the true sport of casino goers: the slots.

The Sport

1. Playing Field: A professional casino. It's not the same in an amateur setting, such as Casino Night at the Lions Club.

2. Players: Anyone with more than $10 and a desire to throw it away. This is definitely an individual game, although some players may form small groups and go "sharesies." However, actually winning something to share is quite rare.

3. Equipment: A building with a lavish interior with numerous games of chance. Glitz and glitter must predominate. Machines must be able to flash lights, make noise and pay out as little as possible, without alienating the players. Player equipment: chips (used in lieu of actual money), purchased from the casino. Pro Slotters have plastic "charge" cards which replace chips.

4. Rules: Each casino has its own rules. They are enforced by large people with bad attitudes.

5. Object of the Game: Pro Slotters expect to make money. The average player hopes to break even. However, the majority of players simply try to stay within their credit card limit.

"Have you ever been to The Casino?" We're at The Bingo, not winning, so we look up. It's the lady across the table, a kindred spirit who, like us, attends for fun and not profit.

Kris shakes her head. I nod. "I've been to Atlantic City on business," I say. "Ninety percent of the people I saw were in jogging suits, pushing a walker. I didn't fit in."

"No, no. I mean a *trip* to The Casino. With the bus."

"Oh! The bus! That's where they pay for everything and even give you free casino money. Everything is free," says Gladys, reaching over to daub a missed number on my sheet.

Free? Now they have our attention. "Where and when?" I ask.

Early the next Wednesday morning, we join several other ladies and Gladys at the United Church parking lot, pickup spot for the Gamblers Express. We are expecting a bright yellow school bus or the Lions Club 12-seater. Instead, a *proper* bus, a tour bus, with toilets, comfortable seats and tinted glass, televisions and speaker system, and a professional driver, pulls up. We are impressed.

As we get in, it becomes obvious that Gladys is related to half the bus, and she goes to sit with her cousin from up the shore to catch up on all the news.

The passengers are an assorted lot, from a young woman in a slinky black cocktail dress (it looked strange on the bus but great in The Casino) to several great-grandmotherly types who bring their knitting. Food in the form of candies, chocolate bars and mints flows from an endless supply tucked in several large floral shopping bags.

"We'll bring our own next time," I whisper to Kris.

"Why bother?" Kris whispers back. "There's plenty here."

Since the mean age of the bus occupants is around sixty, we have a potty break at Webber's in Lake Charlotte, about forty-five minutes down the road. Tim Hortons isn't on the schedule, so we take advantage of their coffee shop and get our caffeine levels back up.

We pull up in front of The Casino. Immediately they separate the sheep from the goats. Those who had been to The Casino before are allowed to get off. No doubt they have the secret password already.

Robert, pronounced *Robair*, is Mr. P.R., complete with canned jokes and clip-on tie. He's the casino representative, official bus-greeter and novice player welcomer. He schmoozes the little old ladies to perfection. We all love it.

Finally, he gets down to the nitty-gritty: a free meal at the buffet, free five dollars worth of tokens, free drink, and a free bet on the Maritime Millions Machine. We can hardly wait.

Each of us is given a temporary ID card that admits us to The Casino. "On your next trip," he says, "you'll be given your permanent card and that will mean you're eligible for all kinds of promotions and events."

"The last time I was promised so much free stuff was in the Publishers Clearing House envelope," I whisper to Kris.

We meet up with Gladys, turn in our chit and receive a bucket full of free nickel tokens. "That's a hundred free games," I say. "You only get forty games with the quarter tokens."

"Yes, but you win more," says Gladys.

"Win more what?" Kris laughs. "We can't even win a simple bingo game."

We head for the slot machine banks. The rows upon rows of glittering, humming, clanging machines are a little daunting. "Let's start with Monopoly," suggests Kris. "That's a game we all know. How hard can it be?"

We stand in front of the machine for several moments. Nothing looks familiar. "Where's The Boardwalk?" I wonder.

"Or Park Place?" adds Kris.

We decide Monopoly, casino-style, is way above our skill level.

"Maybe we should start with something that has lemons and cherries and things. I've seen those on television."

Eventually, we find the lemons and cherries machines. Unfortunately, they are two dollar machines, and Gladys kindly points out that we have to look for the nickel machines. I didn't think it was going to be this complicated. We wander for some time, clutching our untouched buckets, until finally we find a bank of nickel machines.

No cherries or lemons, but a choice of Martians, Hillbillies, Haunted House, Pirate Treasure, and Car Races. We each sit down in front of a machine, but it is heavy going. Every now and then, one of the machines lets forth with a loud bell, whistle, siren or "dum-di-dahHH," and tokens pour out. Unfortunately, we have no idea what we'd done to deserve this bonus. Mostly, the machines just gobble up the tokens.

Before we hit rock bottom, we decide to drown our sorrows at the free buffet. The dining area is like stepping into another world. The ceiling is made to look like a sky that fades and moves and drifts from dawn to sunset, to stars, to dawn. The buffet is lavish.

"Ahh," says Kris, picking up a plate and heading for the mussels. "Now, this is something I understand."

We spend a happy hour noshing and chatting with other folks from the bus. In fact, we debate just staying here, enjoying the ambiance and working our way through the desserts. I can't believe such an elegant place is smart enough to serve bread-pudding-and-custard for people like us.

"If you think this is elegant, wait until you see the Ladies Room," says Gladys. "It's really nice."

She's right. Marble everywhere, free tissues, hand lotion and mints. "We could be in the Ritz Hotel," says Kris, pocketing a few mints.

We decide to stroll around and take a good look at everything. It's much less garish than we thought a casino would be, despite the flashing lights and machine noises. It's even more civilized at the blackjack tables. We watch for several minutes. Our bus companion in the black dress is seated at one. She seems to be winning, if the chips in front of her are any indication. It is very low-key, not at all like the immediate excitement of the machines. We decide it looks boring and head off to a small room separated by glass walls.

"That's for the big gamblers," says Gladys. "The minimum bet is a hundred dollars."

We stand with noses pressed to the glass, watching in awe as one woman drops token (one hundred dollars!) after token (one hundred dollars!) into a machine. Our nickel tokens seem even smaller.

"Ahh, a hundred bucks or a nickel, it's the same thrill," says Kris.

I'm not so sure. Seeing the big money reminds me that we have tokens for the Maritime Millions Machine. The huge story-high monster looms over the room.

"Put in your token," says Gladys. "You could win a million dollars."

"Let's go sharesy," suggests Kris.

"Like The Bingo," says Gladys with a smile, no doubt remembering that so far, the best we've done is share a twenty-five-dollar win.

"I've figured it out," I say. "That's three hundred and thirty-three thousand, three hundred and thirty-three dollars and thirty-three cents each. What'll we do with the extra penny?"

"Let's give it to Robair," Kris says. "For a tip."

No surprise. Robair doesn't get his tip.

"We've still got a few tokens left," I say. "Let's get our free gingerale and blow the bucket."

We find a row of machines that have a seaside theme. They feel comfortable. We know about shells and boats and fish. We settle in for the remaining half hour before the bus leaves.

At the end of the day, I leave with what I arrived with – nothing. Gladys isn't telling, but we fear she's lost a little. And Kris is up $5.50. A pretty good return on someone else's investment.

The oldest of the great-grandmothers, Prudence, is the big winner. As well, she wins the doorprize – a T-shirt and tote bag from The Casino.

At the Lake Charlotte pit stop, Kris tries to call John to let him know we're going to arrive home earlier than we thought. She can't get through, but several ladies promise to call him when they get home. The bus stops frequently from this point on, dropping off weary slotters along Highway 7. Even so, we arrive in Sheet Harbour an hour ahead of when we'd expected to be there.

John is waiting. He'd received three calls from unknown women telling him to be at the United Church parking lot.

"We should do this again," says Gladys.

"Yeah," I agree. "Maybe we need to practice more."

"Not me," Kris point out smugly. "I don't need to practice. I doubled my money."

"It wasn't your money. You doubled their money and kept the change," I remind her.

"We'll have to use our own money next time," Gladys points out. "They only give the free stuff to new players."

"Oh well, let's forget it. I'll never win with my own money. I'm going to quit while I'm ahead," I decide.

"Should I let you know when the next bus trip is?" asks Gladys.

I look at Kris. She looks at me. "Ok," we say in unison.

Two more slotters are born.

Having been born on the other side of the Atlantic Ocean, I confess to having a different perspective on casinos. The word, for me, conjures up mental images of Cary Grant and James Bond, in impeccable evening wear, playing baccarat and roulette with an air of world-weary nonchalance. Our kind of Las Vegas-style casinos with rows of slot machines makes me think of arcades, or seedy pubs in run-

down suburbs of London. I can't make up my mind if people wearing blue jeans and cardigan sweaters, shoving plastic nickels into overblown juke boxes at 2:30 in the afternoon, makes it less like gambling and sort of ok, or just plain weird.

Are You Up For It?

1. Would you rather:
a. "Do" the Cabot Trail on a mountain bike.

b. Crouch in a rubber dinghy, clutching a slippery paddle, dodging rocks and white water spray.

c. Peer through the fog for a glimpse of a whale's tail.

d. Sit on a comfortable stool, sipping a cool drink, and seeing three cherries click into place before your eyes.

2. Would you rather listen to:
a. Pipers piping endless pibrochs at the Highland Games.

b. Screams of terrified riders on the fairground Ferris wheel.

c. The roar of the crowd at a rock concert.

d. The sound of quarters hitting the bottom of a plastic tub.

3. Would you rather waste $25 on:
a. Tickets to the tractor pull.

b. A one-way trip on Confederation Bridge.

c. A used lobster trap to put on top of your car.

d. A bucket of tokens that can only be used in one place and will be gone in twelve minutes.

4. Would you rather watch:
a. The final game of the Stanley Cup Playoffs on television.

b. The dragon boat races in the harbour.

c. The wrestling match between Hulk Hogan and The Abominable Ape.

d. The highrollers blowing $1,000 on a single spin of the roulette wheel.

5. Your idea of a real marathon is:

a. Running twenty-six miles in New York with 3,000 other runners.

b. Swimming the English Channel.

c. Bicycling in the Tour de France.

d. Sitting in front of a "hot" slot machine for 12.4 hours.

Scoring

Simple: Any "d" score indicates someone who is a candidate for the bus trip to the local casino. Sign up today.

As for the rest of you, seek professional help immediately.

Seven Simple Suggestions For Successful Slotting

1. Wear loose underwear. You don't want a "wedgie" while sitting in front of the hottest machine in the Casino.

2. Before playing, loosen your collar and turn back the cuffs on your shirt. This frees up the arm for maximum leverage.

3. Support hose is a good idea if you tend towards swollen ankles. Unlike a plane trip, you won't want to leave your seat and walk around every hour.

4. Use a "fanny" pack and leave your bulging handbag in the bus. Your hands need to be free at all times.

5. Carry some emergency rations – hard candies are best – just in case you feel faint.

6. Don't wear shorts. The seats in front of the slot machines are plastic covered. Enough said.

7. Be sure to bring lip balm. The atmosphere is dry from the air conditioning and the excitement means that you'll be biting/licking your lips frequently.

I always thought my business partner was one of those guys who never gets too excited about anything. We went to Las Vegas for a convention, and he fell hard for the blackjack machines. Every time I saw him, he was parked in front of one of the monsters, totally oblivious to everything around him. I had to keep reminding him of why we were in Las Vegas. Then he disappeared for long periods of time, and I couldn't figure out where he was. Just as we were about to leave for the airport to catch our flight home, he ducked into the Men's Washroom and said he'd just be a minute. Fifteen minutes later, I had to ask a stranger to please go into the Men's Washroom and find him. He was playing blackjack! I knew they had slot machines all over the place, but I never thought they'd get you in the washrooms, too.

Slotting With The Pros

1. Start with a game you know. If you're not sure how to play, stand back and watch a pro in action.

2. Stick with one machine. Every pro will tell you that eventually, every machine gives up its treasure. The longer you play at one machine, the more likely you are to be there when this happens.

3. Play multiple combinations. The beginners stick with one token and one line of play. The pros go for several tokens and multiple combinations of winning lines.

4. Keep conversation to a minimum. The focus is on the machine, not the neighbour next door.

5. Don't overtly have fun. You can enjoy yourself, but don't let anyone see it – no giggling, loud laughter, raucous comments or jumping up and down (especially when you win).

6. Don't let them see you sweat, cry, gnash your teeth, or throw yourself down on the floor (especially when you lose).

7. Don't kick the machine.

8. Drink sparingly. If you're one of those people who fear dehydration and carry a water bottle with you everywhere, see The Number One Secret of the Super Slotter.

> "The best and fastest way to learn a sport is to watch and imitate a champion." – Jean-Claude Killy, alpine skier

The Number One Secret Of The Super Slotter

Wear *Depends*. Yes, really. You can't leave a "hot" machine about to give up its burden of $25,000 just because you have to tinkle.

Skill Building Exercises

Five Things You Can Do At Home
To Become A Better Slotter

1. Eye/Hand Coordination: It's important to be able to put a token into the machine without looking down, and scan the combinations on the screen at the same time. Practice by:
a. Shelling peas while watching television.

b. Cutting your toenails while reading a book.

c. Knitting an afghan while watching the ballgame.

2. Endurance: Good slotters can sit in one spot without moving for hours on end. To help you achieve this state of altered consciousness, practice by:
a. Watching the Parliamentary Channel on television without a snack/potty break.

b. Driving from Halifax to Saint John. Ditto the snack/potty break.

c. Going for a dental appointment and arrive at the correct time. Remain until your name is called, without a snack/potty break.

3. Finger flexibility: At the end of a long day of slotting, flabby fingers can be very painful. Pro slotters never miss hitting the winning combination through finger fatigue. Practice by:
a. Calling everyone on your telephone list and hang up when they answer. Save the news for a letter; just keep dialing.

b. Commandeering the remote for an entire evening of TV and change channels without stopping.

c. Defrosting everything in the freezer by using your microwave oven. Pay special attention to flexing your fingers between each number and command.

4. Concentration and Focus: It's easy to be distracted by other winner/losers, laughing/sobbing around you. Pro Slotters never let their surroundings distract them from the game at hand. Practice by:
a. Going to a local construction site and reading a book.

b. Going to the Emergency Ward of the hospital and taking a nap.

c. Riding the school bus and doing the crossword puzzle.

5. Emotional Control: You'll never know how a Pro Slotter is feeling. Their poker faces and stoic postures give nothing away. Practice by:
a. Watching the complete *Hallowe'en* series of movies without flinching.

b. Watching Walt Disney's *Bambi* without crying.

c. Watching the Three Stooges without laughing.

Glossary of Terms

Bucket or Tub: Container for your tokens. Usually made of plastic like a small margarine tub, but without the lid. Don't put your tub down anywhere – unattended tubs are fair game.

Machine: The big, noisy, shiny things in row upon row upon row. Not all machines are created equal. Look at the price on top – a two-dollar machine does not take nickels!

Token: As good as money in a casino. Tokens come in different denominations, and are not interchangeable. You get them from the counter. You can also trade them back in for real money, in the unlikely event that you either win some or have some left before the bus leaves.

Game: The varieties are endless. Some are familiar, like Monopoly. Some are traditional, using bells, cherries and lemons. Some are weird – Haunted House, Buried Treasure. All have basic rules – put in the token and choose the line to win – but each has its own little quirks. For example, in Buried Treasure, a black pearl in the clamshell means money!

Combination Play: You can win with three of a kind, called one line. Or you can win with a number of combinations, but this costs more tokens. You choose from the keypad on the machine.

Slotter: Anyone who plays a slot machine in a casino.

Super Slotter: Anyone who plays a slot machine in a casino and wins.

High Roller: Anyone who plays the ten dollars and up slot machine in a casino.

Jackpot: An unlikely and rare event when the machine regurgitates a lot more money that you've put in, and signals this by sirens, whistles, bells and flashing lights.

"Half this game is ninety percent mental." – Danny Ozark, Phillies baseball team manager

Instant Replay

The Casino is the extreme sport for you if you:

1. Don't expect to win, but just go to have fun.

2. Can sit still and do one thing for long periods of time.

3. Have very good bladder control.

Degree Of Difficulty For This Sport

A piece of cake – laughable, really, a child under four years old could play this.

If I can do it, you can do it – a child over four years old could play this.

Anyone can do it – you have to pay attention some of the time.

☺☺ Brain cells are used – you have to think some of the time.

Don't try this at home – experienced sporters only.

How To Find This Sport

Look around. If you see a big building with "Casino" in neon lights on top, you've found it.

The Farmers Market Foray —
An Extremely Bucolic Sport

Bucolic:
a. relating to, or typical of, rural life.

Although most food stores have large produce departments, there's nothing like the real thing; at least, that's the consensus of those who regularly shop at the various Farmers Markets in the Maritimes.

Maybe it's buying humongous heads of lettuce with dirt still clinging to the roots, or a dozen brown eggs still warm from under the hen, or a loaf of crusty unsliced bread bursting with whole-wheat kernels, or even smiling back at the freshly-scrubbed farmer's child who is wrapping up your pound of un-salted "real" butter that makes the Farmers Market experience appeal to almost everyone.

Or maybe it's an innate memory thing, regardless of race or culture. At one time or another, we all had ancestors who either sold at the local market or bought there. Doing the same today gives us a sense of connectedness to the past.

Or maybe it's because everything is a lot cheaper and tastes a lot better at the Farmers Market.

The Sport

1. Playing Field: Large, open area either indoors or outdoors, accessible to large numbers of people. Washrooms are always nice. Food is not an option

2. Players: Two teams. The Home Team, usually called "The Producers" – may be farmers, gardeners, crafters, bakers, picklers, jelliers, knitters, butchers, carpenters, quilters, cooks and canners. The Visiting Team, usually called "The Consumers" – may be anyone with a desire for something homemade or home-grown.

3. Equipment: Producers bring what they produce. Consumers bring the usual Visiting Team equipment: cash, cheque book or credit cards.

4. Rules: Producers must offer items that are homemade or home-grown. Freshness is a must. The Consumers must travel in their appropriate group. Consumers may not mix with a group other than their own. (See below).

5. Object of the Game: To buy and sell top quality products, not found in local supermarkets or stores. This is one sport in which both teams work together to achieve a sell-out situation by a pre-determined time. In a perfect game, everything will be sold before the close of play.

My mother used to tell me how she sold her homemade apple jelly at the Farmers Market in a small village near our farm. This was in the late 1940s. She was proud that she charged, and got, $1 a jar. This was a lot of money for that time. Thirty years later, I made up a batch from her "secret" recipe and took it our local Farmers Market. I charged $2.50 a jar, and they went like hotcakes. I had a regular business for some time, but we eventually moved to another area. My daughter used the recipe last year, took hers to the Farmers Market in Saint John and boldly charged $5 a jar. She sold out in the first two hours. People at Farmers Markets know a good thing when they see it and are willing to pay for it, too.

The Visiting Team: Player Profile

In order to maximize your chances of participating in a perfect game, it is vital that you identify your particular consumer niche and appear on the field at the appropriate time. Failure to do so will not only lessen your chances for an enjoyable game, but will also result in confusion to both Home and Visiting team members.

A. The Early Birds
Time Frame: 7–8 a.m.
Profile: Usually loners, often vegetarians, health-conscious, serious shoppers, highly organized and disciplined (no impulse buying here). Sport environmentally correct shopping bags (no plastic), often come on bicycles, distinctive in appearance (highly individualistic in dress), not talkative, do not work in groups, do not stop for a coffee break.

B. Seniors Couples
Time Frame: 8:30–10 a.m.
Profile: Usually in pairs or may join with others to make larger groups. Very social, interact with the stall-holders, generally make one round to pick up regular purchases, and then browse freely. Usually stop for prolonged coffee break, with or without breakfast. Very upscale in appearance: L.L. Bean and Dockers. One suspects a BMW in the parking lot. Some stroll over from nearby condos.

C. Family Packs
Time Frame: 10 a.m.–12 noon
Profile: Combine Market Sport with trips to the library, lunch at Macdonalds, educational outings, etc. Usually children are under 10 years, almost always one in back pack and/or stroller. The group sticks together. They may greet others, but don't join up. Shopping is varied and eclectic. Very prone to impulse buying. Treats are always purchased for the children.

D. Tyros, Teens, and Tourists
Time Frame: 12–closing
Profile: Casual drop-ins, just browsing, looking for entertainment. Purchasing is incidental to the experience. They socialize among themselves but not with others. The Tyros show their inexperience by protesting that "everything has been sold already." The Teens buy little but tend to gravitate to crafts stalls selling wish bracelets and Oriental incense. The Tourists are most likely to buy handmade items.

"He's a guy who gets up at six o'clock in the morning, regardless of what time it is." – Lou Duva, boxing trainer.

"Why don't we just get a hotel room nearby?" I say. My mind is still reeling at the notion of a 4 a.m. departure.

"That'll eat up all our profits," Pat protests.

"Better broke than broken," I say bitterly, but I can see that Pat has no intention of blowing even a dime of her hard-earned money on a hotel room. I resign myself to staying up all night.

At 4 a.m., she's there, bright and cheerful and ready to roll. Thank God she's driving. I sleep most of the way in to town. Pat nudges me awake as we pull into the market parking lot. It's barely 6 a.m., and I'm aghast to see so many cheerful people unpacking huge loads of lettuce, spinach, beets, carrots, beans and potatoes. "Cheerful" seems to be the watchword here: they're calling back and forth to each other, jokingly talking about each other's wares and generally having a good time. At 6 a.m. It isn't natural, I think.

"Coffee?" I croak.

"Unload first," says Pat firmly, no doubt remembering how easily I'm lured by coffee.

I'm too stunned to protest.

It takes us a few minutes to find our booth (table), part of a square of about twelve tables, cheerfully pointed out to us by one of the regulars. "Why is everybody so damn cheerful?" I grumble, glowering at the cheerful lady's piles of hand-knitted potholders and jar upon jar of pickles, jams and jellies.

"Great," says Pat, ignoring me and looking around us. "Location, location, location."

We're steps from the Food Court – coffee, bakery, and breakfast goodies. Even better, we're right in front of the huge glass windows that look out across Halifax Harbour. This has one drawback. We're directly in the line of fire for the incoming ferry.

"I think they wait until they see the whites of our eyes before they veer left into their berth." Pat and I are transfixed as we watch one of these behemoths bearing down directly on us. Only a few panes of glass separate us from certain death.

Sure enough, at the last moment, it turns and disappears from view. By morning's end, we nonchalantly ignore all oncoming vessels.

We settle in, coffees in hand, and look about us. Everywhere, we see tables piled with garden produce and food. We can hardly believe that all this will sell in just one morning. The table to our right is stacked with loaves of bread. We look around and see several other tables similarly stacked with bread.

"They'll never sell all that," I whisper to Pat.

On the other side of us, two ladies are carefully setting out dip samples complete with various corn chips and tortillas.

"Well, at least we won't starve," Pat says, strolling over to sample their wares. She brings back a large corn chip loaded with dip for me.

Behind us, inside the square formed by our group of tables, we're boxed in, literally, by crate upon crate of lettuce and beets, spinach and carrots from the other tables in our small area. In the rest of the market area, produce is stacked against the walls, lines the walkways to the doors and fills the parking lot.

The majority of stallholders are Mennonites. We admire their healthy good looks, but don't envy the women's fitted dresses and caps, or the men's heavy trousers and long-sleeved shirts.

"Now I know how Jezebel felt," says Pat, trying to tug her shorts down over her legs. "I feel almost naked."

It's now 7 a.m. I go for breakfast and return with a scrambled egg on a muffin and another cup of coffee. The crowds are starting to pour in, but it soon becomes obvious they have no interest in our stall of craft goods. They pass us by, their string bags bulging with onions and bread. We notice that they don't even slow down at the coffee shop.

"I hope the rest of the morning isn't going to be like this," I say, watching the bread and spinach piles around us diminish rapidly. Our table remains untouched, but then, so does the dip 'n chip table.

Pat heads off for her breakfast and comes back with a huge spanish omelette and toast. She brings me another cup of coffee. I'm beginning to feel awake and almost alert.

We notice that the crowd is subtly changing. Grey heads predominate, along with Tilley hats and Rockport shoes. People stop and chat and the noise level goes up considerably. The coffee shop is doing a booming business. The little tables in front are full. Our booth finally gets some attention and we make a few sales. Even the chip 'n dip booth is busy.

Pat decides to celebrate with baklavas from a nearby stall. She brings me one, and another cup of coffee.

We each take a bite. Pat goes back and buys half a dozen more to take home.

Slowly, the seniors disappear and we are inundated with the shrill cries of little voices, punctuated with "don't touch that," and "stay near Mommy." Strollers block the aisles, most with a basket full of library books and swimming gear. The pace is much slower, with time for browsing and chatting. Pat, not being a kid person, heads off to the library.

"You can take a break later," she promises me.

By 12, the kids are gone, and Pat is back. We contemplate whether or not we should call it a day. The bread table beside us is sold out, and so are many of the produce stalls. But the chip 'n dip table says they're sticking it out until the bitter end, so we decide to hang in.

We're glad we do because the late crowd likes what we have. Teens in packs, tourists complete with cameras and credit cards, and the inexperienced people who don't realize that the early bird gets the worm at the Farmers Market are all glad to see we're still there.

As well, competition with the piles of produce is no longer a factor. We're pretty much the only game in town. We notice that the chip 'n dippers are doing well, too.

By 1 p.m., it's all over. It takes us only a few minutes to pack up. We've made a small profit.

"Lunch at the Pub or The Vines?" asks Pat, counting out her change.

I check my cash. "The Pub. And next time, let's not come until 10:30," I add.

> "We didn't lose the game; we just ran out of time." – Vince Lombardi, football coach

Going to the Farmers Market here made me remember going to one, long ago, in a small town in the far north of England. Dozens of stalls were set up in the Market Square, where a weekly market had been held for hundreds of years. The only difference now-a-days was in the greatly increased variety of wares offered. True, the stalls were still piled with vegetables and local farm produce, including live animals and fish from the nearby ports, but unlike earlier times, the whole square was ringed with a solid phalanx of trucks, with hucksters on every tailgate shouting the virtues of their imported products. These showmen delighted the crowds by tossing whole tea sets of cheap china into the air, pulling out magician's hats full of sheets and towels, and hacking off dripping hunks of steak from sides of beef, while roaring insults and rough jokes to their audience below. The most amazing thing to me was the contrast, the colour of it all. The town itself was a dark rusty red. The buildings, streets, grass and stunted trees, even the air itself were all red, stained by pollution from the local iron works. The brilliant market lay in its centre, as if a basket of children's toys had been emptied onto a rust-red rug. The vivid jumble of the event wrenched the dull, monochrome town to vibrant life, one day a week.

Instant Replay

The Farmers' Market is the extreme sport for you if you:

1. Believe that the early bird gets the worm.

2. Like to see your food in its natural state.

3. Want to impress your guests with "free range eggs" and "organic carrots."

Degree Of Difficulty For This Sport

A piece of cake – laughable, really, a child under four years old could play this.

If I can do it, you can do it – a child over four years old could play this.

☺☺ Anyone can do it – you have to pay attention some of the time.

Brain cells are used – you have to think some of the time.

Don't try this at home – experienced sporters only.

How To Find This Sport

Get up very early on Saturday morning and follow the crowds.

The Festival Circuit –
An Extremely Profitable Sport

Profitable
a. yielding advantageous returns or results.

Every Maritime community wants in on the tourist business. However, not all of them have sparkling beaches, casinos, heritage sites, whales or water slides. They have to be more creative.

One of the more popular ploys is a Festival – The Blueberry, The Seaside, The Clam, The Maple Syrup, The Strawberry, The Balloon, The Folk, The Covered Bridge, The Bluegrass, The Kite, The Antique Autos, The Tulip, The Dory Boat. You name it, it can be a Festival. Or, if the word "Festival" is taken, it's "Days," as in Pioneer Days.

Having devised a festival, enterprising communities milk it for all its worth. Stores run sidewalk sales, clubs run beer gardens, auxiliaries have bake sales, and the health unit usually has the ducky race (if a river is handy).

The best money spinner of all is food. Festivals like The Clam or The Strawberry dictate what kind of food will be served, but the more generic festivals leave themselves wide open for every organization in town to put on a lunch, barbecue, supper or picnic.

For many small communities, the Festival makes more money than a government grant.

The Sport

1. Playing Field: Any community in the Maritimes with anything that can be made into a celebration: historic event, food item, natural wonder, any object, proximity to water, or renowned personage.

2. Players: Two teams – the Home Team and the Visiting Team.

3. Equipment: Resources of an entire community for the Home Team. The Visiting Team requires cash, cheque books and credit cards.

4. Rules: The Home Team: must provide a valid excuse for a Festival. The Visiting Team: must attend the Festival.

5. Object of the Game:
The Home Team: acquire as much money and fame as possible for the community.
The Visiting Team: participate as much as possible in the event by eating, drinking, dancing, marching, singing, watching, spending, experiencing, listening, learning, and laughing.

"If people don't come out to the ball park, who's going to stop them?" – Yogi Berra, Major League Baseball player and coach and most quoted sportsperson in the world

We know what hell is like.

It's the Church Chowder Luncheon during the Seaside Festival in the middle of August on the hottest day of the summer in the small Masonic Hall kitchen with fifteen hot bodies and eight stove burners blazing under bubbling cauldrons of chowder and the window doesn't open, the fan doesn't work and the door has to be kept closed because of flies and the tourists are lined up six deep at the front clamouring to get in and eighty happy eaters are demanding more hot coffee, while we all hope and pray that the water doesn't run out as it did last year!

The night before is even worse.

There are ten of us, armed with chopping boards, sharp knives, and peelers. The heat is appalling, and the chef has very high standards as to the size and shape of the finished product – minuscule cubes of potatoe, carrot, celery and onions. It take us over two hours to reduce forty pounds of potatoes, twenty pounds of carrots, thirty heads of celery, and ten pounds of onions to the required dimensions. Just in time, the chef stops the celery crew – we're overstocked and don't need to do them all. The fish is already cubed, we're told, and we thank God for small mercies. By the time it's over, we're all in tears – we'd left the onions until the last.

We arrive early on The Day, armed with flowers for the table and a large fan. I volunteer to cut up the desserts. For some reason, most people shy away from this chore, saying they never know what size to make the pieces. This isn't a problem for me – large pieces, of course. But the real reason I always get onto the dessert gang is that I can lick the pans once the pieces are out. In fact, I seldom want much lunch at these affairs, being already replete with chocolate cake crumbs, lemon pie crust bits, carrot cake icing scrapings, cream tart dribbles, and any odd bits of fruit that fall out of the pie.

Kris and I volunteer to be waitresses. Again, most people shy away from this chore, saying they're afraid of spilling things on the customers. Frankly, I figure this is a risk the customer should be prepared to take. After all, we are amateurs.

But the real reason we always volunteer to serve is that we'll do anything to stay out of the kitchen.

The luncheon is slated to begin at 11:30 a.m. By 11:10, the take-out trade is doing a roaring business at the back door.

We finally open the front door at 11:15, and the sit-down crowd is lined up to the road. We know we still have a few minutes before our work begins because every person is encouraged to buy raffle tickets on boxes of groceries (heavy on cans of creamed corn and peas, and this year, bristling with heads of our surplus celery) and various craft items. These are strategically placed next to the ticket table. The hot seller is a basket of "roses," each flower cunningly made from the page of a discarded Bible, tastefully trimmed with iridescent green and pink velvet leaves, and embellished with gold ribbons. We can hear the "oohs" and "ahhs" from the back of the room. "Perfect for Granny in the Home," says one lady, buying a fistful of tickets.

Kris and I split the duties on "our" table, one of the three set up: I serve and she clears. We agree to switch half-way through. A group of six at the first sitting lingers on, no doubt thinking this is like a fine restaurant where conversation over the coffee is *de rigeur*. I long to tell them that the standard practice at these affairs is to chow down and get out because there are people waiting for the seats. They ignore Kris's hints. Even taking away the cream and sugar makes no impact on them.

"Oh well," says Kris. "Makes our job easier, but I had to turn away "real" tourists who were in a rush and couldn't wait. That hurt."

By noon, Kris and I notice that we're now waiting on two of the three tables. We don't know what happened to the ladies assigned to Table #1. They just aren't there. Our leisurely pace is now a thing of the past. So is our division of duties. We both slop soup, clean-up, re-set, stack dirty dishes and find refills of rolls, butter, cream, sugar, and biscuits, for sixty seats.

"Never mind," I tell her as I wipe the sweat dripping off the end of my nose. "This'll look good on a résumé. I've always wanted to be a waitress in hell."

The rush slacks off by 12:45. People are still trickling in and take-outs are still going out, but the pace is much easier. Just as well, because Table #3 has lost half of its staff and we are now responsible for eighty seats. Chowder, with or without lobster, or chicken barley soup, go and get your own dessert, do you want coffee now, oh, let me get you some more rolls, ooops, I'll get a cloth, let me just put a clean napkin over that, where are the cups and saucers, we need more spoons, the slop bucket needs emptying, are you sure you're not going to eat that, are you finished with that bowl, yes, of course, you can have a second helping, yes, it *is* hot, isn't it? It all blurs together.

By 1:15, we close off Tables #1 and #3. By 1:30, it's over. We've pulled in over $1,000. This is a success.

"Next year, let's work in the kitchen," says Kris.

"You got it," I agree.

Because now, we know what hell is like.

> "You learn you can do your best even when it's hard, even when you're tired and maybe hurting a little bit. It feels good to show some courage." – Joe Namath, National Football League quarterback

I kept telling the ladies that I hadn't ever waited on tables before, but because I was young and nimble, they were determined to put me to work. The place was pretty crowded, but I managed to finally get the hang of it. Then, as we were clearing away the dessert dishes, I was working in a particularly narrow aisle between two tables packed with people. I leaned over a lady and picked up her plate and fork. The plate still had a few pieces of blueberry pie on it. As I swung it up over her head, someone behind me jostled me, and the fork started to slide off the plate. I quickly tilted the plate the other way, but went too far, and the bits of pie fell off, landing neatly on her shoulder and then sliding slowly down her back to wedge between her and her chair. She was wearing a white suit. I remember standing there for the longest time, wondering if I should tell her or not since she obviously didn't realize what had happened. I'm not going to tell you whether I did or not. Suffice to say, I never volunteer to wait on tables. I'd rather wash dishes.

Festival Switchback

The game for every member of the family for those rare weekends when there are no festivals in the Maritimes.

Rules: One dice is needed and a marker for each player.

Each person takes a turn throwing the dice.

First one to reach the "finish" wins.

That's it. Good luck.

START	You're at the Jiggleneck Junco Spotters Jamboree. You guess how many jelly beans are in the jar. Go forward 3 spaces.	You're at the Blueberry Grunt Festival. The Grunt is still on the stove. Miss a turn.	You're at the Crunchy Cove Clam Festival. You forgot your clam diggers. Go back 2 spaces.	You're at the Tractor Pull & Farm Life Festival. You find $5 stuck in a hay bale. Go forward 3 spaces.
You're at the Dragon Kite Festival. Another kite eats your kite string. Throw again and move on to the next festival.	You're at the Covered Bridge Days. You win a gas barbecue in the Lions Club raffle. Go forward 3 spaces.	You're at the Blunderbuss Bay Bluegrass Festival. The Foggy Horn Boys do a third encore. Miss a turn.	You're at the South Sluice Strawberry Festival. You get sunstroke and have to spend the afternoon in the First Aid Tent. Miss a turn.	You're at the Fiddlers Neck Sand Castle Festival. You forgot a bucket and spade. Wait 1 turn while you build your castle with a spoon
You're at the Seldom Go By Valley Apple Blossom Festival. You win the apple pie eating contest. Miss a turn until the antacid kicks in.	You're at the Ducky Race at the Deep River Festival. Somone boxes you in at the parking lot. Wait 1 turn until the owner or a tow truck shows up.	You're at the Oldtimers Fiddling Festival. You find front row seats for the Patriarchs Parade. Go forward 2 spaces.	You're at the Rocky Road Maple Sugar Festival & Horse Pull. It's too cold for the sap to run. Throw again and move to the next festival.	You're at the Peaceful Hollow Quilters Festival. The lineup for the Johnny-on-the-Spot is so long you miss the appliqué demonstration. Miss 1 turn.

You're at Middle Dimly Dreamer Days. You're given a free hot dog. Go forward 2 spaces.	You're at the Gravel Grove Groundhog Festival. The groundhog sees his shadow. Miss 2 turns while you wait for spring to come.	You're at the Batters Bridge Annual Beef BBQ & Baseball Playoffs. You get a home run. Move forward 3 spaces.	You're at the Banong Chocolate Lovers Festival. You arrive at the lunch after the fudge is sold out. Take another turn and move on to the next festival.	You're at the Malingerer's Bottom Multicultural Festival. You make a politically incorrect remark about the perogies (food). Miss a turn.
You're at the 50-Mile Yard Sale from Upper Shenanigans to Little Griffle. You cause a 16-vehicle fender bender. Go back 1 space.	You're at the Wooferville Sheep Dog Trials & Festival. You forgot to get film for the camera. Go back 5 spaces.	You're at the Binghamtom Barbership Quartet Festival. You get the wax contract for the mustache-growing contest. Go forward 2 spaces.	You're at the Upper Sporranville Highland Games. The piping band is attacked by blackflies. Throw again and go to another festival.	You're at the Lower Tickle Trout Derby. The big one gets aways. Go back 2 spaces.
FINISH	It rains all weekend. Go back to START.	You're at the Chapstick Crossing Corn Growers Festival. You break out in hives after the chicken plucking contest. Miss 1 turn until the rash subsides.	You're at the Lumberjacks Festival. You're the 1,000th visitor and are given a free axe and a cord of firewood. Go forward 3 spaces.	You're at the Cuddlewick Oldtimers Campfire Days. Your entry starts a small brush fire at the main event. Wait 1 turn while you put it out.

Years ago the only festival around here was the village Flower Show. The money went to things like the hospital and there was coffee and tea and cookies, and stalls with games like hoop-la and such for people to spend their money on. You paid to put your flowers and vegetables and quilts and canning and wood-carving and things into the competitions. I suppose it was something like the Agricultural Show, but we never got to that because them days hardly anybody along the shore had a car.

Glossary of Terms

Festival: any excuse for an event to draw in visitors and entice them to spend their money in your community.

Days: any excuse for an event to draw in visitors and entice them to spend their money in your community.

Fair: any excuse for an event to draw in visitors and entice them to spend their money in your community.

Jamboree: any excuse for an event to draw in visitors and entice them to spend their money in your community.

Carnival: any excuse for an event to draw in visitors and entice them to spend their money in your community.

Derby: any excuse for an event to draw in visitors and entice them to spend their money in your community.

Games: any excuse for an event to draw in visitors and entice them to spend their money in your community.

Homecoming: any excuse for an event to draw in visitors and entice them to spend their money in your community.

Show: any excuse for an event to draw in visitors and entice them to spend their money in your community.

Ceilidh: any excuse for an event to draw in visitors and entice them to spend their money in your community.

Kitchen Party: any excuse for an event to draw in visitors and entice them to spend their money in your community.

Contest: any excuse for an event to draw in visitors and entice them to spend their money in your community.

> "It's designed to break your heart. The game begins in the spring when everything is new again and it blossoms in the summer, filling afternoons and evenings, and then as soon as the chill rains come, it stops and leaves you to face the fall alone." – A. Bartlett Giamatti, Commissioner of Major League Baseball, 1989

Instant Replay

Festivals are the extreme sport for you if you:

1. Have a particular interest in the subject of the festival.

2. Enjoy activities with lots of participants.

3. Haven't anything better to do on the weekend.

Degree of Difficulty For This Sport

☺☺ A piece of cake – laughable, really, a child under four years old could play this.

If I can do it, you can do it – a child over four years old could play this.

Anyone can do it – you have to pay attention some of the time.

Brain cells are used – you have to think some of the time.

Don't try this at home – experienced sporters only.

How To Find This Sport

Listen to people boasting about their hometown which has the biggest/oldest/best/nearest/famous/notorious/historical _____ (fill in any object, person or place) in the country, and they have a festival to celebrate it.

The Real Estate Chase –
An Extremely Bold Sport

Bold:
a. intrepid
b. showing or requiring a fearless, daring spirit,
c. impudent, presumptuous, assured, confident.

In the winter, the locals put out apples to attract the deer for hunting. In summer, they put out "For Sale" signs to attract the visitors for buying. The visitors come, they look, and they dream of that little cottage by the sea.

The Sport

1. Playing Field: The Maritimes.

2. Players: Three teams: those who have property to sell, those who have a dream of buying it, and those who act as the middleman (the real estate agent).

> "In the summertime, I'm not a real estate agent; I'm a tour guide." – Maritime real estate agent

3. Equipment: An advertisement in the newspaper or real estate guide. Alternately, the advertisement can be a hand-written sign in the supermarket or a piece of cardboard attached to a tree. A "For Sale" sign, preferably on the property in question.

4. Rules: *Caveat emptor* – buyer beware.

5. Object of the Game:
The Seller: unload the property at the highest possible price.
The Buyer: buy the dream property at the lowest possible price.
The Real Estate Agent: work both ends against the middle and come out with the highest possible commission.

"Summertime, and the real estate is sellin'
Suckers are buying,
And the prices is high..."

Pat is extemporizing as usual as we barrel along the road in search of the fourteenth perfect "hideaway by the sea" this morning. We're out scouting for some Ontario friends who have a yen to retire to Nova Scotia.

Today, we're on the trail of a small parcel of oceanfront that advertised itself with a crude hand-painted sign on the side of the highway. We'd called the number and now we're on our way to see this seaside gem.

"She said to go down the driveway and it's on the shore," Pat says, as we slow down and peer for a driveway.

"There's a driveway near the sign," I observe. "That must be it."

We pull in and park just off the highway.

To the left, the sign seems to indicate that the land is the lovely open forested area along the shore.

"Looking good," says Pat, plunging in. "Not too mossy and someone has limbed the trees not so long ago. It won't be hard to build in here."

I follow her and admit that this is one of the nicest spots we'd seen. "How come it's so cheap?" I wonder out loud.

"Well, it's not with a real estate agent. Probably the lady has no idea how much it's really worth."

"Yeah, and her boyfriend said it would never sell."

"Which is how much he knows about Nova Scotia ocean-front real estate." We both grin and look smugly at each other. It looks like we've struck gold.

"Oh-oh. There's some kind of shed or something on the shore."

"But it's supposed to be vacant land," I say indignantly. Sure enough, there's an old trailer, up on blocks and once painted a vivid blue, now peeling and streaked with rust.

"Yuck! What an eyesore! It's going to cost to have this thing hauled away."

"We won't have to pay. We'll just get the guy who put it here to take it away. He's poaching on someone else's land." We walk around the trailer to the shore.

The shore is lovely, with a road along the edge. "Wonder what this road is?" I say. "She never mentioned a road, did she?"

"No. She said you went down the driveway, along the shore a bit, and the land was right there."

We stand silently for a moment, trying to get our bearings.

"I don't think this is it," I say. "We didn't come down the driveway, we went through the woods. But there is a road here, so let's go along the shore and see if there's another sign."

The beach is lovely, and we're delayed for quite some time as we load up with driftwood and shells. Finally, we pull ourselves away and head down the beach and around a small headland.

"Uh-oh. This is somebody's front yard." Pat looks back at me. "There's only a swamp between it and the old trailer."

"You don't think the land is the swamp, do you?" I have that sinking feeling.

"No, no. It's not big enough. The piece is three acres, she said, and this doesn't even look like an acre," Pat says. "Let's backtrack and start again."

We head back to the car, get in, and begin to slowly drive down the edge of the highway. The land is here somewhere, we know that, but the question is, where?

"There's another driveway just here," I say, pulling in. "But it's gated, and there's no sign or anything."

"Just a minute. Let me think about what the owner said. I know she said something about going past someone's house and then turning... right! Not left, but right, along the beach. We went left before. We were at the wrong end."

"But we couldn't turn right back there. There was a cottage and then nothing."

We stand and survey the gate.

"We could walk around it," I suggest. "There's probably no one here if the gate is locked."

We squeeze around the gateposts and start down a muddy, rutted, narrow, overgrown lane. About fifty feet in, the lane disappears underwater where a culvert has collapsed. Fortunately, we always wear our gummy rubbers on land explorations so we just slosh through. It's too early in the year for mosquitoes and blackflies, although we could tell this would be prime breeding grounds later on.

Around a bend, we come upon a newly re-sited construction hut with the company name and logo still visible underneath a thin coat of white paint.

"Instant cottage," says Pat, "and look, a cosy outdoor fireplace."

"That's an incinerator," I say disbelievingly. Right in front of the window, between the cottage and view, is a huge, rusting incinerator.

"Let's not speculate on what they do for entertainment."

We pass the "cottage" and come up to a small, disintegrating trailer with its sheet metal walls peeling off to reveal soggy bats of insulation and panelling inside. The whole thing is sunk into the ground and what is left of the deck is just rotting timbers. Two old refrigerators and a car wreck adorn the shore.

"No doubt waiting for high tide to take them out," suggests Pat.

The yard is criss-crossed with four-wheeler ruts. We begin to get a feeling that this might not be all that we hoped.

"Now, we just turn right and there's supposed to be some kind of marker."

"Yuk! I found it!" Pat backs up, looking disgusted.

In front of us is a wood pile made from old driftwood logs and trees. On top of one crooked branch is a deer head, an old trophy, now with only one antler and one eye. The eye watches us balefully.

"Abandon hope all ye who enter here," I mutter, edging around it.

On the other side of the deer head is another hand-painted "For Sale" sign, placed so that it faces the ocean for the purpose of attracting the nautical trade. Just beyond the sign is a sagging outhouse, minus a roof and door.

"This must be the little building she mentioned." We peer inside. "A two-holer! Wow! Now that's togetherness."

"Is it still usable?" I wonder. "With a door and roof replaced, of course." I peer tentatively down one of the holes. The unmistakable gleam of water tells me that the drainage leaves a lot to be desired.

We walk down to the beach. It's like a little rounded point, with several huge rocks just made for sitting and thinking. A grove of tall spruce off to one side is ideal for a picnic table.

"What a view! I wonder why the boyfriend thought she'd never sell it."

"It's gorgeous," I agree. "Let's look for a building site."

We turn from the beach and push back beyond the fringe of spruces and immediately sink up to our knees in a bog.

"The irises are nice," says Pat. "You wouldn't have to plant a garden."

I lose my boot. It takes me several minutes to wrestle it back from the bog. I now have a wet foot and I'm not interested in the irises.

The bog goes back the full length of the lot and ends in a thin fringe of moss-draped, dying trees. In places, it goes from bog to swamp, complete with little pools and frog spawn.

"Perhaps a little place on stilts."

"Or pontoons," Pat says, picking Spanish moss out of her hair.

"The boyfriend was right. She'll never sell it."

"At least not to us."

"Let's go look at that other piece I told you about."

"*Summertime, and the wishers are dreaming,*
That the next lot
They look at is fine…."

I pick up the tune,

"*Facing south, looking out to the ocean,*
Maritimes,
And the price is a dime…"

> "I wouldn't ever set out to hurt anybody deliberately unless it was, you know, important – like a league game or something."
> – Dick Butkus, National Football League linebacker

There's a personality test game that has you describe your dream home. The kind of house and its environs seemingly tell things about the type of person you are. It's kind of fun, as long as you don't take it to heart. The only trouble is that it's like being asked your favourite colour. Mine's yellow unless I happen to be looking at a clump of iris, or a fresh mackerel, or an old fire truck or something, it's hard to settle. One day I'd really love to live in a stone croft by the sea. The next time anyone asks it could be a log A-frame in the forest, or a penthouse apartment overlooking Halifax Harbour. A white farm house with painted shutters on PEI would be nice, or something Victorianish covered in gingerbread down around Saint Stephen. Thinking even bigger I could go for a red brick Queen Anne manor house with white stone corners and a knot garden. In fact when it comes to real estate choices it's pretty much wide open. I'll look at anything.

Glossary of Terms

Oceanfrontage: theoretically, there is some shoreline. However, there is oceanfrontage, and then there is *"oceanfrontage."* The descriptive word is the clue to what you're buying.

Bold oceanfrontage: directly looking out to the open ocean. Heaven on a calm, sunny day in July. Hell in hurricane season.

Tidal oceanfrontage: only available at low tide, and then, muddy.

Harbour oceanfrontage: crowded waterfront shared with sewage outpipes, marinas and various personal watercraft.

Outer harbour oceanfrontage: the same, but further to go to the store.

Sea meadows: these are salt marshes, also known as reeds in mud. They look lovely, especially in a picture, but you can't walk on them and you can only use them for your boat at high tide in the summer. One good thing: they usually freeze in the winter, so they're great for snowmobiles.

Sloping to the beach: a high cliff.

Gently sloping to the beach: a low cliff.

Access to the beach: you have to cross the road and go down a flight of steps.

Access to the beach: you have to go through someone else's yard.

Access to the beach: you and sixty other homeowners have a narrow right of way to a 50-foot stretch of communal beach.

Access to the beach: there's a public beach or provincial park somewhere within a 20-mile radius.

Distant view of the Atlantic: if you're in the bathroom, standing on the toilet seat, in the winter, at sunset.

Road is in: someone has driven a bulldozer through the thick spruce bush.

Power nearby: there's a power pole somewhere within a 20-mile radius.

Perked: you have permission to put in a septic system. This doesn't mean that there's water available or that it will be easy to put in the system. Always ask, "Where was it perked?" Sometimes the perk site is within a 20-mile radius of your chosen building site.

Shingle beach: small rocks.

Bold beach: big rocks.

Sand beach: tiny rocks.

Active beach: comes and goes with the tides. Today, it's a sandy area at low tide. Tomorrow, it's back to shingle (see above). If the beach is backed by a high crest of rocks, ask, "Has this moved in the last five years?" Chances are, it has, and is continuing to move, directly onto your new piece of land and eventually, your septic system.

Deep anchorage: deep water within a 20-mile radius.

Wharf: any structure of any size that goes out any distance into the water.

Boat house: garage that was built near an active beach.

Then there's the house. What you see in the pretty coloured real estate ad isn't necessarily what you get.

Hand-hewn beams: Uncle Pete built it.

Many recent upgrades: Uncle Pete fixed it up.

Original woodwork: Great Uncle Pete built it.

Restored: *Oncle Pierre* fixed it up.

Heritage: so old we can't remember *who* built it or fixed it up.

***Needs T.L.C.*:** this used to be called a "handyman's special," but now that there are "handywomen," this is more politically correct. Bottom line: it will be cheaper to pull it down and build a new house.

Executive home: looks like a suburban transplant from Toronto.

Fisherman's cottage: built right on the road with sixteen sheds between the house and the ocean, blocking all possible view of the water. Note: they built boats, not houses. Be prepared for an upside down boat. They're solid, they don't leak, but the interior finishing leaves a little to be desired.

Captain's house: same as above, but bigger and usually overpriced.

Heritage home: usually in a town and must conform to the historical society guidelines for buildings in the area. Don't plan to put on new aluminum siding.

Quaint: small and inconvenient.

Hideaway: twenty miles down a dirt road.

Surrounded by trees: impenetrable forest all around.

Open: not a tree in sight.

Private: same as hideaway (see above).

More or less: when you see this in any description of land, beware. It means they don't know what the exact dimensions are, have no way of finding out, and hope that no one else will claim the land. It also means that the land can come and go according to the tides (see "active beach" and "sea meadows" above).

Negotiable: the seller is desperate.

"In twenty-six years in the pros, I haven't noticed many changes. The players are faster, bigger, smarter and more disloyal to their owners, but that's about it." – George Blanda, AFL/NFL player.

I was so excited when I read the ad. It said five acres on the ocean with a house that needed some work. The price was really low, but I presumed that was because the house was currently used to store fishing gear. Anyway, we drove out to take a look. The property was alongside a small river that emptied into the ocean and it was very picturesque, with a little bridge and everything. Well, the house was pretty bad all right, but what worried us was the land behind the house. It seemed low and boggy, but we could see a fence on the far side, so it must have been used as a pasture at one time or another. A day or two later, we decided to come back and have another look before we made an offer to the real estate agent. What we didn't realize is that we'd seen the house at low tide the first time. This time, it was high tide. There wasn't any land behind the house at all! Just water stretching across a little bay, and on the other side, the fence line we'd seen before. We very nearly bought five acres of tidal swamp."

Are You Ready For The Sport Of Real Estate?

The ad reads: *Modest home showing pride of ownership on 20 acres +– with greenhouse, potting shed, double car garage, wood shed, artist's studio, boathouse, gazebo and guest cottage.*

Does this mean:
a) Every room in the house is painted and wallpapered within an inch of its life. If it's not moving, it's decorated.

b) It's an old farm by the ocean with twenty acres on which are buried twelve cars, several farm implements and more tires than you can count.

c) It has numerous outbuilding and sheds between the house and the ocean.

d) All of the above.

The ad reads: *"Executive ranch on 2 beautiful acres, richly forested, with oceanview."*

Does this mean:
a) A bungalow with aluminum siding and phony shutters.

b) Impenetrable forest all around.

c) A swath has been bulldozed between the back of the house and the ocean.

d) All of the above.

The ad reads: *"Perfect site for your dream house by the sea. 5 acres on a commanding bluff with breathtaking views of the bold ocean. Sleep with the sound of waves at night."*

Does this mean:
a) A 60-foot high cliff plunging down to massive boulders below.

b) There's nothing between you and Ireland.

c) The shorefront is known locally as "The Devil's Cauldron."

d) All of the above.

The ad reads: *"Victorian gem, fully restored to its former grandeur, in a quaint seaside village on a quiet road. Easy access to all services and numerous sand beaches."*

Does this mean:
a) It's Victorian all the way: 20-amp power, no telephone lines in, lath and plaster walls, no shower, no dishwasher, and no closets in any of the twenty-two rooms.

b) The village is a well-known tourist trap on the main route along the shore. From May to October, traffic is non-stop and usually backed up for several miles.

c) There is a gas station on one side and a Tim Hortons on the other. The Atlantic Superstore is across the street. The sand beaches are within a 20-mile radius.

d) All of the above.

If you answered "D" for all the questions, you're ready to hit the road on the quest for that perfect piece of the Maritimes.

"Facing south, looking out to the ocean,
Maritimes,
And the price is a dime…"

> "I'm too lazy to work and too scared to steal." – Tom Bolton, Major League Baseball pitcher.

The only thing I'm not allowed to inspect with a view to purchase are vacant lots. My husband knows only too well that I'd never be able to make up my mind what to build on it.

Instant Replay

The Real Estate Chase is the extreme sport for you if you:

1. Believe everything you see written.

2. Believe that someone wants to sell you a mansion for a dollar.

3. Believe that your dream home actually exists.

Degree of Difficulty For This Sport

A piece of cake – laughable, really, a child under four years old could play this.

If I can do it, you can do it – a child over four years old could play this.

☺☺ Anyone can do it – you have to pay attention some of the time.

☺☺ Brain cells are used – you have to think some of the time.

Don't try this at home – experienced sporters only.

How To Find This Sport

Look for a sign that says "Property For Sale."

The Home Sales Party Match –
An Extremely Expensive Sport

Expensive:
a. commanding a high price and especially one that is not based on intrinsic worth or is beyond a prospective buyer's means.

In the long, cold, dark nights of winter, a Maritime tradition is the home sales party: plastic tubs, clothing, leather, candles, lace, jewellry, cosmetics, lingerie, silk plants, wickerware, Christmas decorations, and spices. You name it, you can buy it at a home sales party.

The premise is that it is an opportunity for friends to gather, share a little food, and have some fun. The bottom line is you're there to buy something so that your hostess can get a gift. There's no such thing as a free lunch at a home sales party.

The classier parties have wine and cheese; some even throw in a luncheon. Most offer chips and dip and coffee. Since the amount you spend is predicated on the quality of the food offered by the hostess, the wise hostess has learned to ply you with Strawberry Zinfandel. After three glasses, you'll buy anything.

The height of social acceptance in the community is to be invited to all the home sales parties. Generally speaking, if you're known as a "good" buyer, you'll get invited. The end goal of the hostess is to provide as many warm bodies as possible for the sales pitch, so she'll often invite family friends and relations to fill up the room.

However, there is some discrimination when the product has a certain "*je ne sais quoi.*" We're still wondering why no one has yet to invite us to a Sexy Lingerie Party.

The Sport

1. Playing Field: A living room or basement family room, no larger than 12 by 12. Must contain at least twelve chairs plus a sofa, as well as a table for merchandise displays. A space for players to put food, drinks, catalogues or forms is optional. However, a separate, discreet area must be provided for the salesperson to write up orders.

2. Players: Two teams. The Home Team is a pairs team: the sales representative and the hostess. The Visiting Team can number from one to thirty and is made up of anyone who is inveigled to show up with the promise of free food, drink and a little entertainment.

3. Equipment: Pens, order forms and catalogues, plus sample merchandise provided by the sales representative. Suitable re-fresh-ments provided by the hostess. Cash and credit cards provided by the Visiting Team.

4. Rules: Each member of the Visiting Team must buy something, however minimal, in payment for the free food, drinks and entertainment.

5. Object of the Game: see Cosmic Battle below.

Do You Have A Home Sales Party Personality?

Score the following statements using:

     1 – Not at all like me. Also known as "over my dead body,"

     2 – Somewhat like me. I might.

     3 – Occasionally like me. I've been known to.

     4 – Usually like me. Whatever.

     5 – Very much like me. You bet!

1. When the gang gets together, I do most of the talking._____

2. I like to join in the conversation and get my two cents worth in. _____

3. I like to take charge. _____

4. If it's a choice between getting together with people or watching a rerun on t.v., people win. _____

5. I expect my friends to be entertaining. _____

6. People call me a "party person." _____

7. I like to tell people how to run their lives. _____

8. I'm the "hostess with the mostest." _____

9. I'm good at getting other people to do things. _____

10. I'll go places where I don't know anyone. _____

11. I like to find out everything about people and don't mind asking questions. _____

12. I enjoy mixing in a crowd. _____

13. I'm known as a bundle of energy. _____

14. I make friends very easily. _____

15. I talk a lot. _____

16. I stick by my friends, no matter what. _____

17. I like things to be organized, and if they aren't, I step in and take over. _____

18. I have no problems having fun at a gathering. _____

19. If I'm in charge, everybody knows it. _____

20. I like to chat with people. _____

21. I can talk anybody into anything. _____

22. I let it all hang out with my friends. _____

23. I usually end up running the show. _____

24. I don't like quiet gatherings. _____

For the following questions, give yourself a 5 if you answer Yes, and a 1 if you answer No.

25. Someone makes a really stupid remark. You know he or she is wrong. No one else seems to have noticed. Do you correct the person in front of the others? _____

26. After a hard day's work, would you rather party than stay home? _____

27. Are you usually the one who comes up with the great party ideas? _____

28. When you want to celebrate, do you have a party with a gang rather than a small, intimate dinner? _____

29. If you have a problem with someone, you confront them, rather than doing nothing and hoping it will resolve itself. _____

30. Most people think you're an extrovert. _____

Scoring

Add up your scores for the odd-numbered questions: _____

Add up your scores for the even-numbered questions: _____

A higher odd-numbered score indicates that you are a more likely to take the hostess role rather than that of a guest.

For each score, find your Home Party Style:

For the odd-numbered questions:

15–33: You're probably invited to every party in the community, and you probably always buy something you don't want. Bottom line: you can't say "No."

34–56: You get invited to lots of parties, but you feel free to decline the invitation, and not to buy if you go. You have a balanced view of the Home Sales Party.

57–75: If you go to the party, you always sign up to be the next hostess because you know you can do a better job. You prefer to run your own party and you always end up with bonuses and extra gifts when you do. You're a natural for the Home Sales Party Hostess. In fact, you're a natural for the Leader of the Home Sales Team: you could sell plastic tubs at a Greenpeace Convention.

For the even-numbered questions:

15–33: People don't bother asking you to their Home Sales Parties anymore. If you do get dragged along, you sit apart from the rest, don't play the silly games, and never buy anything.

34–56: You get invited to lots of parties, but you feel free to decline the invitation, and not to buy if you go. You have a balanced view of the Home Sales Party.

57-75: You love the Home Sales Parties. You never miss an opportunity to go, and you don't mind spending money on the products. If you do end up hostessing one, everyone comes, and everyone has such a great time, they never get around to buying anything.

> "If winning isn't everything, why do they keep score?" – Vince Lombardi, National Football League coach

The Cosmic Battle Between The Forces of Resistance And Compulsion Or The Ying And Yang Of The Home Sales Party

You're there for a good time: food, fellowship and fun.
They're there to persuade you to part with your money.

Five Proven Tips To Help You Win The Cosmic Battle

1. Encourage other people to buy. If you can get a feeding frenzy started, no one notices that you haven't bought anything yourself. It's a diversionary tactic that always works.

2. Demand it in an impossible colour or size. Talk it up, mention how wonderful it is, remark on the workmanship, the quality, the price, but oh dear, if only they had it in puce, chartreuse or aquamarine in size double XX. (Warning: be sure you check the catalogue before using this ploy. You'd be amazed what colours and sizes are available these days.)

3. Be disarmingly frank about your finances. Tell everyone that you don't have any money. Blame your partner, your kids, your mortgage, your job, your lay-off, your health… anything will do. People are so embarrassed by your frankness, they won't push any further.

4. Have someone call you right after the lunch and the demonstration is over. So sorry, but you have to leave immediately. Give no explanations: just get out of there. If anyone asks later, say that your long lost uncle was calling back long distance from England, and you had to get home.

5. If all else fails, buy the damn thing. Then send it back. (Note: make sure they have a money-back guarantee).

> "Baseball is the only sport I know that, when you're on the offensive, the other team controls the ball." – Ken Harrelson, Major League Baseball player

I nearly got into the home sales business once. I thought it might be easier than having a real job. For once, I actually thought about it carefully first. It didn't take very long for me to realized that there might be more to it than met the eye. There was all the driving around in the dark trying to find strange places in bad weather. Then I'd actually have to buy a lot of stuff up front before making a penny to pay for it. Add to that my knack for forgetting things, and presuming that all the things I need are in the bottom of my purse, when they're not, and you can see why I decided not to do it. Lugging huge boxes in and out of cars, taking orders and delivering the right stuff to the right people, doing math and dealing with irate customers – not likely. Almost any real job I'd be likely to get would be a lot easier.

The invitations arrive in the mail. Immediately, we know this is a cut above the usual Home Sales Party where invitations are just part of the casual conversation in the grocery store. If someone is willing to spend forty-eight cents on stamp, it must be good.

It's for clothing, and since there is no clothing store in the nearby village, we figure it's an excellent opportunity to avoid a trip to The City.

There are nine guests plus the hostess and the Sales Rep. One side of the room is taken up by two large clothing racks stuffed with knitwear. Kris and I give each other the nod – this is looking better all the time, especially when the hostess offers us a large glass of Peach Chardonnay and passes a plate of cheese puffs, and all this at two o'clock in the afternoon.

"Eat up," I say. "You won't have to worry about supper."

"I hope she serves coffee, or we'll have to walk home," Kris answers, accepting a top-up on her glass.

We settle back for the presentation. This is standard procedure at these parties, and we expect to see hangers of clothing held up for our inspection. Much to our surprise, the Sales Rep, a woman of our age and build, proceeds to perform the most intricate and dignified strip-tease we've ever seen.

At no time do we actually see anything remotely inappropriate (beyond a bra strap), yet she manages to get in and out of sixteen different outfits and combinations in half an hour. We are enthralled by her performance.

The sales pitch is low-key. She makes sure we know the bottom line in dollars required for the hostess to receive her free gift. She also suggests that we might like to host our own parties. Then she hands out pencils and order forms and announces she'll await us in the kitchen for our orders. We admire her discretion – all sales are seemingly confidential. Later we learn that the sales amounts are shown to the hostess who cheerfully tells others how much each person spent at the party.

The hostess points out the various change areas: bathroom, bedrooms, basement and family room. Everyone surges forward and grabs several garments off the racks. Few actually opt for the changing areas, and we're treated to something akin to the Full Monty right there in the parlour.

At the same time, the food is served: little sandwiches, mini quiches, dips and veggies, and a tray of gooey, rich squares. Kris and I load up.

We join in the chorus of encouragement and praise for the impromptu fashion show as people model their choices. We're good at this, and no one notices that we haven't marked anything on our little order forms yet.

I try on a green outfit. It looked better on the Sales Rep.

"It's not your colour," says Kris. She's trying to get into a pair of blue trousers.

"They're not your shape," I say back at her.

We paw through the racks, and eventually come up with outfits that we like. The stuff is good quality, Canadian made and guaranteed to be wash and wear. The price is high, but then we're saving gas by not going into The City. I'm pleased to find a three-piece outfit that I can travel in: skirt, jacket and trousers in an unusual shade of burgundy. Kris picks out a red dress that can convert to a long skirt. "Good for a beach cover-up, too," she says, admiring herself in the mirror.

We notice that we both look good in this mirror. "I bet this is one of those mirrors that make you look taller and thinner than you really are," I say to Kris, turning around to admire my mirror-svelte behind. "I've certainly never looked this good in a knit outfit before."

"I wouldn't be at all surprised if these mirrors come as part of the sales kit," Kris says, also turning around for a back-end view. We both smooth the knit fabric down over our hips.

Business is brisk in the kitchen and we have to wait in line. It's a good excuse to have some more chocolate squares, and we're glad that the coffee pot is making the rounds.

By four o'clock, we're down several hundred dollars between us, and we still have to wait six weeks before the stuff comes in.

"Never mind," I say, "at least I won't see myself coming in every door. When I shop in the department stores, everything looks the same."

"Yes, that's a really unusual combination you put together," Kris adds. She knows how much I hate to look like everyone else.

As we leave, one of the guests comes rushing up to the car. "I just had to tell you," she says. "I loved the outfit you chose. When I saw it, I went right back and changed my order. I'm getting one just like it."

When we get home, I call the Sales Rep and cancel my order. I haven't been invited out a lot since then.

I remember the first time my Mom took me to a Home Sales Party. I was about ten years old, and I was so excited to be included in a grown-up event. It was held at my Aunt June's house, and there were about a dozen neighbours there. I was the only kid. The party was for Tupperware, and everyone was oohing and ahhing over all the new stuff. Then the sales lady showed us how to "burp" our bowls. She gave me one and let me try it. I remember the feeling of pride and satisfaction as I made my bowl "burp." From that moment on, I was sold. I never miss a Tupperware party. I bet I have every piece of Tupperware that's ever been made.

Instant Replay

The Home Sales Party is the extreme sport for you if you:

1. Know that there's no such thing as a "free lunch."

2. Like playing silly games and winning a bar of lavender soap.

3. Are easily persuaded to buy.

Degree Of Difficulty For This Sport

☺☺ A piece of cake – laughable, really, a child under four years old could play this.

If I can do it, you can do it – a child over four years old could play this.

Anyone can do it – you have to pay attention some of the time.

Brain cells are used – you have to think some of the time.

Don't try this at home – experienced sporters only.

How To Find This Sport

Don't do anything. They'll find you.

The Indoor Flea Market Hunt – An Extremely Comfortable Sport

Comfortable
a. affording or enjoying contentment and security,
b. free from stress or tension.

Sunday shopping is still a point of contention in the Maritimes. Unlike their sister provinces in the rest of Canada, the Maritimes still considers Sunday a day of rest. That doesn't mean you can't shop; you can, but only in designated stores. How "they" decide to designate a store as Sunday-shopping friendly is beyond us. For awhile, we had to skirt roped-off areas in our local grocery store if we shopped on a Sunday. Meat and dairy were off-limits; canned goods were okay. Or was it the other way around?

However, Maritimers like to shop. So, to get around this legal issue, the Indoor Flea Market, usually held in a mall, fills the Sunday gap. For a nominal entrance fee, you can browse for hours in air-conditioned comfort. If you don't feel up to home-made wontons and samosas from one of the booths, you can nosh on the commercial version of the same thing at the Chinese Wok in the Food Court. If you're not into ethnic food, there's always A&W. Better than the Johnny-on-the-Spot at an outdoor flea market, the spacious mall restrooms are open for your business.

Although there are the regulars, the majority of the vendors come and go. You'll find trading cards, videos, used books, antiques, oil paintings done on the spot, 'fresh' flowers, fudge, pies, ethnic foods, clothing, sunglasses, pet supplies, hand-crafted pine furniture, painted rocks, driftwood clocks, shell wreaths, jewellry, watches, toys, electronic equipment, sunhats, cell phones, soap, candles, quilts, knitted goods, and numerous one-time vendors who obviously don't have a garage or yard for their sale and bring all their unwanted items to the flea market.

It's a great way to spend a rainy Sunday.

The Sport

1. The Playing Field: Any mall that does not have Sunday shopping. The field can also be any building with a large indoor area. These are usually set up on a permanent basis and keep regular business hours.

2. Players: Two teams: Buyers and Sellers. To determine which team you should be on, complete the quiz below.

3. Equipment: The Seller Team provides something to buy. The Buyer Team provides cash, cheque books and credit cards.

4. Rules: This is a relaxed version of the Craft Fair. The game is shorter and less intense. Basically, Buyers can buy if they wish; Sellers can also buy from other sellers, or simply socialize and enjoy the day.

5. Object of the Game: To sell a little; to buy a little; to eat a little.

Which Side Of The Table Should You Be On: Buyer or Seller?

Unlike most sports, where there are doers and watchers, the Indoor Flea Market offers opportunities for participation in two distinct ways. This sport has two players: the buyer and the seller. The line between the two is narrow and frequently overlaps. However, to get the most enjoyment from the sport, it helps if you know your natural bent.

Choose your most likely response to the following statements. If you're torn between the two, go with your first inclination.

1. You see something on a vendor's table that appeals to you greatly. You pick it up, look at it, think about it and...
a. Decide to buy it even though you have something similar at home because they would make a nice set.
b. Decide you have something similar at home, and maybe it's time to gather up a load of your junk and take a table next Sunday.

2. You look at a jumble of displayed goods on the table and...
a. Poke around until you find what you want and buy it.
b. Imagine how you're going to set up your display when you take a table next Sunday.

3. You see a table display of homemade fudge and...
a. Try some and tell the vendor your grandmother's recipe is better.
b. Try some, then go home and root out Grandma's recipe and make some to sell next Sunday.

4. You look at a table loaded with yard sale junk and...
a. Decide there's nothing here worth buying.
b. Mentally calculate how much money they're going to get for it, double this amount in your mind for your superior junk at your table next Sunday.

5. You see a table with craft items and they're not selling very well, so you...
a. Buy one to make the vendor feel better.
b. Make an offer for the whole lot, take them home, add some dried flowers and ribbons, and sell them at an enormous profit on your table next Sunday.

Scoring

Mostly A answers: you're an entrepreneur's dream. Keep on buying!

Mostly B answers: you're a true entrepreneur. Selling is your sport.

> "You don't play people. You play a ball. You don't ever hit a guy in the butt and knock him over the net – unless you're really upset." – Vic Braden, tennis player.

We're sellers.

The table is only $15 she tells me. That's $7.50 each, I figure. Do-able. Until Pat tells me what time we've got to leave the house in order to be there on time.

"Six! You've got to be kidding!" I gape at her.

"Well, we have to be there by eight, or they'll give our table to someone else. That means we must leave no later than six. I'll drive. You can sleep on the way in."

I'm unconvinced and feeling pale. Why does everything we do involve an early morning start?

We leave at 6:15. Nothing like a time pressure to add edge to the morning. However, it's dawn on a Sunday morning, so there's no traffic. Not even a logging truck. We're there in record time.

"We'll set up first," Pat tells me. "Then we'll get coffee from Tim Hortons." I decide that this indoor flea market gig can't be all bad if there's a Tim Hortons nearby.

"That is, if they're open yet," Pat adds.

"They'd better be."

We get our table number and find the right entrance. The place is bustling like a disturbed anthill. Much to our surprise, there are more than 200 vendors, all trying to set up at the same time. The tables range from sophisticated show booths, complete with lighting and drapes, to a plastic tablecloth under a heap of boxes. We're somewhere in the middle range with a few display stands and signs.

After a few minutes of fumbling, we both realize that coffee is a priority. Pat happily trundles off to find Tim Hortons and I continue with the set-up. By 8:45, we're full of coffee and donuts, the display looks great and we've met our booth neighbours on either side, a watch/sunglass king and a trading card mogul.

Our table location is perfect. Right in the middle of the Food Court (how did they know?), underneath the skylight, just across from the washrooms and a major entrance.

"This is comfortable," says Pat, sipping her triple triple. She settles back in her lawn chair and selects another donut. "Much better than those outdoor flea markets with wind, dust, hot sun, or rain, mud and mosquitoes."

"Yeah," I agree. "This is the civilized way to sell. Now all we need is buyers."

They start to dribble in and by 10 a.m. the mall is jumping. Many of the buyers are obviously regulars – they've got their favourite booths and chat with old friends.

"They don't look like the usual mall crowds," I say to Pat, eyeing one woman with numerous shopping bags, and an eclectic outfit which includes multiple necklaces and a shawl.

"Nooo.." says Pat, as a humungous guy covered in tattoos stops at the booth next door.

So far, everyone is looking, oohing and ahhing, but not buying.

"They've got their hands on their wallets," says the trading card mogul. We notice that he's spending a lot of time talking about his card collection, but not much time actually selling. We hope this isn't a trend.

Across the aisle, the "live" artist is working on his second(!) landscape of the morning. We watch in amazement. A central golden circle, spreading out to hues of blue, then bisected with a dark horizontal line that becomes the horizon, and with a few judicious green strokes for trees, he has a perfect sunset/ sunrise with reflection in the water. People are snapping them up. We consider a change of career.

It's my turn to replenish the coffee supply. I come back with coffee, a CD, a lettuce, a dozen roses and piggy-shaped biscuits for my dog.

At eleven, the crowd subtly changes. Now it's families with young children. The mall looks like a busy Saturday in December.

Our sales aren't brisk, but they're not embarrassing, unlike the booth two spots down. Esoteric "artistic" creations of glasses filled with clear plastic, bits of wire, stones and shells, all labelled with names like "Tranquillity," "Oceana," "Inner Thoughts," "Yesterday," and "Dream of the Future." People stop, look, pick one up, frown, and put it back down. They don't buy.

Meanwhile, we're noticing a trend at our table. Men like our stuff a lot; women don't. Unfortunately, it's the women who buy.

"Maybe I should add some flowers and ribbon," mutters Pat, rearranging her items one more time.

"Or throw in free candy," I suggest.

Pat goes for coffee. She comes back with coffee, a tray of peanut butter cookies, a scarf for her mother, two books and a T-shirt for her daughter.

Shortly after twelve, we notice another shift in the crowd. This time, it's older couples, nicely dressed, who are obviously on their way home from church. They drift around, pick up and put down, but don't buy. We soon realize they're there for the Food Court.

Which reminds us, it's time for lunch. I take the first shift. I'm torn: A&W or Chinese Wok. The Wok wins and I bring back a plate of food. Pat heads back to Tim Hortons but has to settle for soup since all the sandwiches are sold out.

Dessert is two homemade eclairs from a booth several stores up.

Now the crowd is made up of folks looking for an afternoon's diversion. Some of them tell us they've come for an outing, driving in from the countryside. We meet two people from Sheet Harbour, and they're as surprised to see us as we are to see them.

"It's such a nice day," she tells us, "we decided to drive in. We often do this."

We try to imagine leaving our lovely shore for a city mall on a nice day.

"We're only here to make money," I tell them. They don't get the hint and leave without purchasing.

"Time for tea," I say, and head for Tim Hortons. I come back with tea, a necklace, a pair of shoes and loaf of homemade bread.

The artist is on his fourth painting. "It's a commission," he tells us proudly. "The client brought in paint samples of her bathroom and wanted something to match." We watch him start with a slighter greyer circle, and we know where it is going.

The sunglass/watch king next to us seems to have pressing business elsewhere. We keep finding ourselves explaining that it's not our table as impatient customers line up to buy the gold/diamond watch/pendant/ring combination or the purple/rhinestone/wraparound sunglasses. We try to lure them to our table, but we can't compete with his glitter.

Meanwhile, the trading card mogul is explaining yet again to another avid crowd of 14-year-olds how the Giant Squid Card with the Sword of Power and Might can overcome the Caverns of Doom and Gloom and eliminate the Dastardly Dragon Fish.... or something like that.

The day is slowly winding down.

"I'll get some Ice Caps for the road," says Pat.

"And some Tim-bits. It's a long drive home."

She returns with two frosty cups, a small package of Tim-bits, plus a bag of fudge, a dried eucalyptus spray, and some knitting wool and patterns. She's wearing a big straw hat with a flower on it.

I say nothing.

It's time to pack. We're done in fifteen minutes and head for the car.

"How come we have an extra box?" I ask Pat. "I thought we sold at least a box-full."

"I put all the stuff we bought in there," says Pat.

Driving home, she totals the sales. "We made our booth and a little bit over," she says jubilantly.

117

"I knew we would." I feel smug. This is a good way to make a living, I think.

"But we're down on gas, food and miscellaneous."

"How much down?" I ask.

"Twenty bucks for gas, twenty more for food, and about thirty each for miscellaneous. Basically, we're in the red for about fifty dollars."

"Yeah," I say. "But look at all the good stuff we got."

Pat agrees.

Perhaps we are buyers and not sellers after all.

> "The first thing is to love your sport. Never do it to please someone else. It has to be yours." – Peggy Fleming, figure skater

They have a flea market every Sunday in this run-down old building on the edge of town. I've been there hundreds of times and I see the same shoppers every Sunday. I know all the proprietors, too, and they know what I like. Nine times out of ten, if I buy an item, it's something they've put aside for me. There's always new stuff to look at. It's the thrill of the hunt, I guess, the thought that you might find a really fantastic treasure under the piles of junk, that brings us out. I just feel like I've missed out if I miss a Sunday at that flea market. Silly, isn't it?"

The Rainy Sunday Flea Market Game

It's Sunday. It's raining. Everything is closed. You can't go to the beach. The kids are whining. The guests are restless. There's nothing on television. No one wants to play cards, and if you have to listen to either the kids squabbling over the videos, or Uncle Sherm telling of his gall-bladder operation one more time, you'll go nuts.

It's a day from Hell.

Now is the time for the Rainy Sunday Flea Market Game.

Equipment

Paper and pencils.

Rules

1. Each player must work alone. Under 10-year-olds should team up with an adult.

2. Points are allocated two ways:
a. The Quick and Easy Game: one point per item
b. The Advanced Game: points are allocated according to difficulty/obscurity of item.

How To Play

1. Each person is given a list of items to find at the Indoor Flea Market. Note: the longer the list, the longer the game. How desperate are you?

2. A time limit is set and a rendezvous is arranged. (We suggest the Food Court).

3. When an item is found, the vendor is asked to sign the list and put in his table number. This way, suspect items can be verified.

4. The highest scorer wins. As host/hostess, your job is to find something absolutely ridiculous/unusual/interesting at the Flea Market as a prize. Set yourself a price limit so you're not tempted to buy the Elvis-on-black-velvet-pillow for $50.

You'll need to make up lists beforehand. Here are two sample lists. One is simple with one point per item, and one is advanced with scoring suggestions.

SIMPLE LIST	ADVANCED LIST
1. Spider Man Trading Card	1. Rocket Richard Trading Card – 5 pts.
2. Walt Disney Video	2. *Breakfast at Tiffany's* Video – 5 pts.
3. Fudge	3. Peanut butter/chocolate fudge – 4 pts
4. Hardcover book	4. Book by Charles Dickens – 4 pts.
5. Green T-shirt	5. T-shirt with Number 12 – 5 pts.
6. Baby clothes	6. Yellow baby dress – 4 pts.
7. Sunglasses	7. Orange, wraparound sunglasses – 5 pts.
8. Dozen roses	8. Dozen yellow roses – 3 pts.
9. Pet supplies	9. Green dog biscuits – 2 pts.
10. Old plate	10. "Royal Albert" plate – 3 pts.
11. Tupperware	11. Tupperware cake taker – 2 pts.
12. Ship model	12. Ship in bottle – 5 pts.
13. Tennis racket	13. Violin – 5 pts.
14. Pair of shoes	14. Golf shoes – 4 pts.
15. Pine shelf	15. Tole-painted shelf – 3 pts.
16. Picture in frame	16. Original oil painting – 4 pts.
17. CDs	17. Eight Track tapes – 3 pts.
18. Afghan	18. Pink/green/yellow quilt – 3 pts.
20. Cell phone	20. Rotary dial phone – 5 pts.
BONUS ITEMS – 5 pts. each	BONUS ITEMS – 10 pts. each
1. In-line skates	1. Roller skates
2. Kid's toy with wheels	2. Kid's wooden wagon
3. Apple pie	3. New York cheese cake
4. Necklace of coloured beads	4. Rhinestone necklace
5. Car Tire	5. Car Radio
SUPER BONUS – 10 pts	SUPER BONUS – 25 pts.
A man's tie with purple stripes.	Any Elvis Presley item

These are just suggestions. Adapt your list to fit your age group and interests. These lists would be for a short game. Fifty or more items pretty much takes care of your family and guests for several hours, especially when combined with lunch and free time for personal shopping!

Note: you can adapt the Rainy Day Indoor Flea Market Game for outdoor flea markets, community yard sales or a yard sale crawl. Some folks do the same thing with a Frenchy's crawl as well.

"To my way of thinking, going to one of those indoor flea markets at the mall is like doing the rounds of the yard sales in the comfort of your own home." Old Grammie Esma is lecturing us as she gets her toenails 'seen to' at the adult day clinic. As she's nearly ninety-eight, she's in a position to tell us just about anything she wants to without fear of contradiction, especially since her son, Young Emmet, a mere sprig of eighty-one, has promised that he won't put her in the Home while she can still make bread. (Not that he got away with that one so easy, since she came right back and told him that if he didn't move his rear end out of her kitchen and dig some potatoes she would put him in the Home for being so cheeky.)

"Only it's a sight better'n no yard sale to my way o' thinking."

"Why is it better, Grammie?" asks Tammy filing away at her gnarled old toes with dedicated concentration. The old lady is paying plenty to get her monthly pedicure these days and she expects value for money.

"All you see now is a pile of junk that they bought from some other yard sale. Time was you got good stuff, right out of people's kitchens and front parlours. And the prices was real reasonable."

She pauses to demand more lotion.

"The stuff they sell now hasn't seen the insides of no-body's house for years. It just goes the rounds from shed to shed, one yard sale table to the next. They got real nice things besides that junky stuff in the mall sale, and there's a place to get your dinner, and a nice bathroom besides. And you don't have to keep hauling your poor old bones in and out of the truck. You can't beat the Market at the Mall."

Instant Replay

The Indoor Flea Market is for you if you:

1. Are "made of sugar" – you melt in the rain.

2. Think a "johnny-on-the-spot" is only for construction workers.

3. Can't bear to miss a day at the mall.

Degree Of Difficulty For This Sport

A piece of cake – laughable, really, a child under four years old could play this.

☺☺ If I can do it, you can do it – a child over four years old could play this.

Anyone can do it – you have to pay attention some of the time.

Brain cells are used – you have to think some of the time.

Don't try this at home – experienced sporters only.

How To Find This Sport

Look for malls with lots of cars in the parking lot on a Sunday.

The Frenchy's Store Crawl – An Extremely Sporting Sport

Sporting:
a. marked by or calling for sportsmanship,
b. involving such risks as a sports contender may expect to take or en-counter.

Shopping at Frenchy's is such a popular Maritime sport it merits its own book on the subject (*The Frenchy's Connection*, Potters-field Press, 2001). The hunt for the Super-Bargain is on a par with a safari into deepest, darkest Africa, only without the bugs. In fact, the sport has gone international, with a Frenchy's Down Under store opening in Australia. Even more exciting, a new Frenchy's store has opened in Newfoundland.

For those who are wondering what we're talking about, Frenchy's is the generic name of a loose chain of used clothing stores in the Maritimes.

The Sport

1. The Playing Field: Any indoor space with low rent. Parking, washroom, windows, lighting, dressing room and elbow room are all optional.

2. Players: This is the only sport in which everyone is on the same team. Anyone can play, male and female, from toddlers to octogenarians. Basically, anyone with $2 and the will to "root" – more later – is welcome to join the team.

3. Equipment: Plastic bags full of secondhand clothing, preferably unpacked and displayed on table tops, clothing racks, in cardboard boxes and heaps on the floor.

4. Rules: If you grab it, it's yours. If you put it down and someone else picks it up, it's theirs.

5. Object of the Game: To find a Super-Bargain, an Oscar de la Renta jacket for $5, or a Dior purse for a buck. Failing this, points are always given for any items purchased that are (a) cheap, (b) in your size, and (c) wearable.

Note: the following excerpts are from our book, *The Frenchy's Connection*.

What kind of people shop in Frenchy's? People like you? Or people *not* like you? It's always a good idea to know where you fit into the Frenchy's universe.

Read each statement and circle the most appropriate response using the scale of 1 to 5 as shown for each section. There are four sections: how you were then, how you are now, your attitudes, and your creativity.

Remember, this is not a life-and-death quiz. No one will see the answers except you. You won't end up in a database, won't be put on any mailing lists, no representative will call, and nothing in a plain, brown wrapper will appear in your mailbox.

There are no right or wrong responses. Don't agonize. Don't go in for internal navel gazing. Go with your first instinctive response. And good luck.

Quiz Section One – Then

5 = Are you psychic?
4 = Well, didn't everyone?
3 = Sorta sometimes
2 = Whatever...
1 = Oh, yuk!

5 4 3 2 1   When I was a kid, I loved to receive hand-me-down clothes.

5 4 3 2 1   I frequently borrowed my mother's or some other adults clothes to wear to school.

5 4 3 2 1   I often came home from school wearing different clothes than I started out in.

5 4 3 2 1   I always believed that my wardrobe is your wardrobe, and vice versa.

5 4 3 2 1   Halloween was my very favourite holiday.

5 4 3 2 1   I knew my boyfriend's wardrobe better than his record collection.

5 4 3 2 1   When an item of clothing went missing, my wardrobe was the first one searched.

5 4 3 2 1   I never missed a program of *Mr. Dressup*.

5 4 3 2 1   If I liked it, I wore it.

5 4 3 2 1   Anything, from my bedspread to a lace curtain, could become an item of clothing.

Quiz Section Two – Now

5 = I'm thinking of seeking professional help
4 = Pretty well all the time, but I know when to stop
3 = It depends on various factors from the phase of the moon to the budget
2 = If I really, really have to
1 = Over my dead body

5 4 3 2 1   I never miss a rummage sale.

5 4 3 2 1   I admit that what I'm wearing is secondhand.

5 4 3 2 1   I buy a bargain even if I know it won't fit, because you never know...

5 4 3 2 1   I know what looks good on me, but I don't let that stand in the way of a good bargain.

5 4 3 2 1   Okay, so my closet is full, but, but I can always find room for one more.

5 4 3 2 1   I'd rather rummage through a pile of used clothing than shop in Holt Renfrew.

5 4 3 2 1   I shop in secondhand stores for gifts.

5 4 3 2 1   I do washing, ironing and sewing on buttons as part of the shopping experience.

5 4 3 2 1   I'd wear a secondhand "buy" to my son's wedding.

5 4 3 2 1   I enjoy rummaging through sagging cardboard boxes full of shoes.

Quiz Section Three — Attitudes

5 = I'm considering starting a new religion
4 = It goes without saying
3 = I'm open to discussion either way
2 = Only in moments of weakness
1 = You've got to be kidding!

5 4 3 2 1   Euphemisms such as "new-to-you," "gently used," "second-time-around," and "second edition" are for beginners. Used is used.

5 4 3 2 1   Clothes are more comfortable after they've been broken in by somebody else.

5 4 3 2 1   It's a waste of money buying new clothes for kids.

5 4 3 2 1   Plush carpeting, soft lighting and accurate sizing do not a good store make.

5 4 3 2 1   Wrinkles and odours are temporary and don't detract from the allure of clothing.

5 4 3 2 1   There's nothing wrong in wearing dead people's clothing.

5 4 3 2 1   As long as the shoe fits, you can wear it.

5 4 3 2 1   Style and fashion are simply a state of mind.

5 4 3 2 1   Designer clothing is designer clothing, whether you buy it new or used.

5 4 3 2 1   Revealing where you buy your clothes is a matter of personal conscience.

Quiz Section Four – Thinking Outside The Bins

5 = Anything goes
4 = Occasional flashes of insight
3 = After my first cup of coffee
2 – I never thought of that
1 = Whah??

5 4 3 2 1   Just because it's labelled curtains doesn't mean it has to hang at a window.

5 4 3 2 1   Just because it's labelled men's doesn't mean a man has to wear it.

5 4 3 2 1   Just because the label says "Bi-Way" doesn't mean that you can't replace it with a spare "Gap" label.

5 4 3 2 1   Just because it's a wedding dress doesn't mean it can't become placemats, curtains or a tooth-fairy pillow.

5 4 3 2 1   Just because it's white doesn't mean it couldn't become orange.

Scoring

Add up the total of your responses for all the questions.
My total is: _____

35-67

We guess you're probably just reading this to investigate the phenomenon of the success of second-hand clothing stores. Perhaps you have a friend that you're trying to help overcome her addiction. That's very noble of you. However, studies have shown that recovery rates are low with this particular problem. Probably the best you can do is just be there for her, with the occasional "oooh" and "aaah" for her latest find.

And thank you. We need people like you to give your lovely used clothing to people like Frenchy's so people like us (and your friend), can keep on shopping. Hats off to you!

68-80

Is it possible that you are a closet Frenchy's shopper? Or are you a wannabe who hasn't had the opportunities to spread your wings and shop?

Perhaps you're one of those unfortunate cases where a higher-than-average income has held you back from exploring the possibilities offered by used clothing. If so, you may find it freeing to think of your used clothing purchases as charitable donations that will benefit so many people. As well, you can give yourself environmental strokes for good behaviour as you embrace the principles of recycling.

Go for it! It's good for you!

81-113

Our hearts go out to you. We recognize your vulnerability. You could go either way at this point. Peer pressure could be a deciding factor. We suspect that you feel torn between two worlds, not yet ready to give up boutique browsing and expresso coffee for Frenchy's and a donut.

Don't despair. You're not alone. Thousands like you are discovering the joy and freedom of a good bin rummage. The movement is growing. Throw off the shackles of tradition and come and join us. Buck the establishment and push the envelope.

We shall overcome!

114-146

You're in this mainly for the thrills. The thrill of that fantastic find. The thrill of telling someone that your designer gown only cost five bucks at Frenchy's. The thrill of diving into a freshly-filled bin, untouched by others. The thrill of discovering a Coach bag in the pile of plastic purses. The thrill of spending the money you save at Frenchy's on a cashmere sweater from The Bay. Ooops!

You're not fully committed to the cause. Although you recognize the advantages of Frenchy's shopping, there's still the lure of the pricey boutique. We understand. You're in the majority of Frenchy's shoppers. Saving at Frenchy's is a means to an end.

Just remember to put that cashmere sweater in a charity bin when you're done with it. It might fit one of us.

147-175

You are over the top! If you recognize your addiction and want to do something about it, here's a quick 12-step program for you.

1. Admit you have a problem and that you resolve to do something about it.

2. Go to your primary closet. Anything that is still in a green plastic garbage bag and hasn't been unpacked is out. Give it to your local charity.

3. Go to your secondary closet (and we know you have one). Repeat the process.

4. Go to the attic. Take out all and any clothing stored there. Give it to your local charity.

5. Go to the spare bedroom. Repeat #4.

6. Go to the basement. Repeat #4.

7. Go to the garage. Repeat #4.

8. Go to the garden shed. Repeat #4.

9. Go to the closets of all other members of your family. Repeat #4.

10. Go to the trunk of your car. Repeat #4.

11. Go to the pantry. Repeat #4.

12. Finally, go to your friends' closets, garages, basements, attics, garden sheds, car trunks and pantries, and any other place where you have asked them to "hold" things for you, and repeat #4.

There. That wasn't so hard was it?

A sorority group came to one of our readings of the *Frenchy's Connection*. They were a riot. They told us that they had a great time at their annual get-together. They played a game. Each member drew a sister's name and was sent off on the traditional Frenchy's crawl to all their favourite local stores to buy clothes for that person to wear to the evening's festivities. Each year they had a special costume theme and since they were only allowed to spend ten dollars each on the outfits, it took a lot of ingenuity and imagination to earn the loudest applause.

"All winning teams are goal oriented. Teams like these win consistently because everyone connected with them concentrates on specific objectives. They go about their business with blinders on; nothing will distract them from achieving their aims." – Lou Holtz, former University of Notre Dame football coach

"O.K. Let's look at the logistics. It's now 9:30 and we have to be back by 4:30. That gives us seven hours. That includes three hours of driving, an hour for lunch and two coffee breaks. Plus driving to and from stores and a quick stop at the mall. There are four good stores in Truro. Can we do it?"

"Sure we can," says Gladys. "When I was on a trip with a gang, we set a time limit for each store."

"I'll be the time keeper," I say. "Synchronize watches everybody." And we're off.

An hour and a half later, we swing into Tim Hortons. "Fifteen minutes," I remind them.

We're in and out like a comfortable shoe. Ten minutes to pick up Elinor, Kris's daughter, and five minutes to Louie's on Willow Street. "Thirty minutes," I announce, checking my watch.

We've missed "two-for-one" Monday, but there are still plenty of good bargains. Elinor picks up a couple of fancy dresses and a pair of shoes to die for. Oh, to be young again! "Five minutes more," I holler. Several shoppers look alarmed.

It's twenty minutes later before we're back on the road. "Now look, guys," I say threateningly. "If we're going to do this, you've all got to cooperate." I fix Kris with a stern look. "Now we have to knock off ten minutes at the next store."

We go to Frenchy's Used Clothing on Meadow Drive – a fairly new building, down a side street that comes dangerously close to the on-ramp for the 102. We wonder how many unwitting Frenchy shoppers have found themselves hurtling up the highway to Onslow with the Frenchy's sign receding in the rear-view mirror.

Everyone is now focused by my threats: no chatting, no frivolous nonsense. Each one goes directly to the bin of her choice and gets down to business. This timing system seems to bring out the best in all of us. Elinor easily fills a green garbage bag with children's clothing. Kris loads up on buttons, I get a couple of cotton sweaters, and Gladys finds a brand new sweatshirt with her daughter's name on it. In exactly twenty-five minutes we're on time and out the door.

We bump into three businessmen, nattily dressed in suits and ties, their late-model cars looking very smart in the parking lot. Businessmen's lunch in Truro, we wonder. Guess they'd rather root than eat, too.

At least my being in charge of the time-keeping means that we will eat at reasonable times. "Lunch time – one hour. Let's go," I say.

The choices are wide on this street of fast food and family restaurants. We settle for Smitty's for the usual reasons: it's on the right side of the road and there's a parking space near the door.

Stuffed with pancakes, bacon and eggs and clutching take-out desserts, we stagger back into the car exactly one hour later. I'm beginning to consider an alternate career as time-keeper at the Olympic games. I seem to have a talent for it.

Another Louie's is just down the street. It's not a place we would normally pull in to, at any time of the day. It looks like a conglomeration of long-defunct businesses in a wooden warehouse badly in need of paint, repairs and glazing. The parking lot is muddy and rutty. We actually hesitate to get out of the car.

"Oh, come on," says Gladys. "I can see lots of people in there. It can't be that bad."

"Remember, half an hour," I warn the others. We figure ten minutes should do it if the outside appearance is any indication of what's inside.

We're wrong. This is a goldmine! Everything from a "Weird Stuff Bin," to a wall of Men's Wear racks, to a mound of amazing underwear, all in several cavernous rooms smelling faintly of mildew and age.

"Ever notice how the good stuff is always in the crummy places?" says Kris, diving into a pile of women's sweaters.

Reluctantly, we drag ourselves out exactly twenty-seven minutes later. We're good, we decide.

It's time for the mall. Each of us has a short list of "must-gets," and since this is the nearest mall to where we live, we can't afford to pass it up.

"Only fifteen minutes," I decide. "We'll meet back here by the door. If you're late, I'm leaving without you." You have to be tough when you're the time-keeper.

In fifteen minutes: I go to the money machine and the Wicker Emporium where I buy a large basket; Kris buys trousers for her mother at Zellers; Elinor goes to the Drug Store and picks up a prescription; Gladys heads for the Dollar Shop and brings back Scratch 'n Win tickets for everybody; and we have time left to Scratch and Not Win.

"Three down, one to go, and we're still on schedule. Next stop – Salvation Army downtown on Prince Street." Kris looks at the map.

"It's not far from here," Elinor says, "but I think there's a lot of one-way streets."

She's right. We pass the same elm-tree stump, carved to resemble a Scotsman in full highland dress, several times before we're finally going in the right direction, on the right street, on the right side.

From the outside, the store looks small, but inside, it's Dollar Daze. We happily root about for fifteen minutes when I realize there are no women's items. I decide to explore and eventually, much like the one-way streets, end up in the right room at the back which has not only women's clothing, but also housewares and linens. I yell for the others to join me.

It's here I find two new suede jackets – one red bomber style perfect for Elinor and one beige shirt-style for me. The clerk cheerfully gives them to me for half price since I'm buying both, and throws in my sweater for free. I think I'll come here again.

Kris finds out that this is an independent store, not part of the National Recycling Organization, but run by the local church.

We all agree, it's a great store. In fact, Truro has been great, too.

It's 2:30. We drop off Elinor and her bags and head home. We're running a little behind schedule, so we get our triple- triples to go – probably not the best idea considering the spring pothole state of the roads. We're all drinking carefully, until I decide to pass a logging truck.

As I'd seen my husband do in similar circumstance, I simply "put my foot down."

The resulting sudden acceleration and G-forces sent Gladys' cup straight up. "Not to worry," she said bravely, mopping coffee off her face, sweater and trousers. "I bought two new pair of pants today. They probably cost less than my coffee and donut."

At precisely 4:30, we pull into the driveway. Are we good, or what?

> "You look forward to it like a birthday party when you're a kid. You think something wonderful is going to happen." – Joe DiMaggio, ballplayer on Opening Day of the Baseball Season

Instant Replay

The Frenchy's Store is the extreme sport for you if you:

1. Hate fancy dress boutiques.

2. Hate pretentious sales clerks.

3. Hate looking like everybody else.

Degree Of Difficulty For This Sport

A piece of cake – laughable, really, a child under four years old could play this.

If I can do it, you can do it – a child over four years old could play this.

☺☺ Anyone can do it – you have to pay attention some of the time.

Brain cells are used – you have to think some of the time.

Don't try this at home – experienced sporters only.

How To Find This Sport

Admire someone's silk blouse or leather purse and ask her where she bought it.

The Card Party Funambulism Forum – An Extremely Awesome Sport

Funambulism:
a. a show of mental agility.

Forum:
a. a public meeting place.

Awe:
a. the power to inspire dread,
b. emotion in which dread, veneration and wonder are variously mingled,
c. wondering reverence, tinged with fear, inspired by the sublime.

Auction, Auction 45s, Cribbage, Tarabish, King Peed, Thirteens, Bridge, Whist, Euchre and Canasta – these are names that inspire dread in anyone but the professional card player. In the Maritimes, cards are a serious business, and players train from earliest childhood by sitting around the kitchen table with various uncles and aunts and playing into the wee hours.

The Card Party is often a fundraiser or a club activity. It's not a place where you learn to play cards. Only the expert players are welcome to participate in this elite sport.

The Sport

1. Playing Field: Community halls, church halls, fire halls, lodges and meeting rooms – anywhere there is room for a number of card tables and a lunch can be served comfortably.

2. Players: Strictly professionals.

3. Equipment: Card tables/chairs/decks of cards/score sheets/prizes/food are supplied by the hosting organization. Players pay to play.

4. Rules: Vary with the game being played. Note: always ask if in doubt since local rules always supercede official rules.

5. Object of the Game: To get through the session without alienating your partner or being told you "don't have the brains God gave a cod" by others. Winning is good, too.

> "We're supposed to be perfect our first day on the job and then show constant improvement." – Ed Vargo, Major League Baseball umpire

I played cards when I was in college. In fact, I spent a good many hours in the cafeteria hunched over a hot hand. But I'd never play cards at one of the local Card Parties, not because I don't know how to play but because of one embarrassing thing. You're probably going to laugh at me, but it's this: I can't shuffle to save my life. Honestly! I've tried to learn and I've even practiced on my own, but I just can't do it. The cards all fall out of my hands and I can feel every one watching me and laughing. I'd kind of like to go to a Card Party, though, but I doubt they'd let me bring one of those automatic shufflers."

Card Skill Levels

Assess your skill level *before* going to a Maritime Card Party.

Are any of these statements true for you?

a) I always lose when I play a game of "Happy Families" with the grandchildren.

b) I think "Snap" is a highly competitive card game.

c) I have trouble counting the combinations of numbers that make 15.

If you answered "Yes" to even one of these statements – Don't Go.

a) I used to play euchre on the school bus.

b) I still like a game of Crazy 8s now and then.

c) I play cribbage with my grandfather.

If you answered "Yes" to even one of these statements – Don't Go.

a) When my brother and I play gin rummy, it can get pretty competitive.

b) I took bridge lessons at evening class last year.

c) I play computer cribbage and often win.

If you answered "Yes" to even one of these statements – Don't Go.

a) I attend a monthly Poker Game with my buddies.

b) My bridge club meets twice a month.

c) My mother and I enjoy a game of Piquet after supper.

If you answered "Yes" to even one of these statements – Don't Go.

a) My grandmother taught me how to play King Peed when I was 5, and I've been playing it ever since. (I'm over 50.)

b) My family likes to get together to play Auction 45s. I haven't spoken to my sister since she made that stupid play at our last game.

c) I was one of the first people who learned to play Tarabish when it first started up in Cape Breton.

If you answered "Yes" to even one of these statements – Go.

"I mind we used to play cards with some friends called Neil and Ione, when we lived up in Cape Breton Island," Cambell said as he got out the crib board. "She was a big lass. Noel was no small man now. But Ione, she stood a good half head taller and she had a pair of — "

"Cambell, watch your tongue!" his wife, Bella cut in sharply.

"Shoulders, woman! I was going to say shoulders."

Bella sniffed suspiciously and poured home-made bits and bites into a bowl.

"Ione MacGregor had shoulders a quarterback would have taken steroids for. Now aren't I right, woman?"

"It's true enough," Bella conceded. "She was a big woman, there's no question. But for all that she was very feminine in her ways. She had lovely hair and she spoke so soft and with a lisp like. A sweet girl was Ione."

Cambell snorted. "Oh aye. Sweet spoken and as daft as a peahen when it came to card playing. I still to this day don't know how she did it. We'd play at Hearts, wouldn't we, woman? Ione scattering her hand and the suits all mixed up. She would always be calling Clubs 'blackberries' in that daft little voice till you felt like choking her. I swear she never remembered what had been played already, or even which way round she passed her cards, but time and again there'd be Noel stuck with the Queen of Spades and Ione winning." He started to chuckle and even Bella, who is one of the dourest people I ever met, couldn't help cracking a small smile.

She nodded, "'Ohh Ioneee!' That was him, moaning when she'd won again. 'Ohh Ioneee!' Then she'd say, 'Stop whining, you great wimp!' all in that quiet little lispy voice of hers, and she'd fetch him the devil of a bang on his arm with her fist. Make him yell too, I tell you."

Cambell dealt the cards thoughtfully. "It can be a violent game, cards you know, can't it, woman?"

Serious sport has nothing to do with fair play. It is bound up with hatred, jealousy, boastfullness, disregard of all rules, and sadistic pleasure in witnessing violence: in other words, it is war minus the shooting. – George Orwell, author

We thought that "45" meant an age limit for the participants. Whether it was under or over 45, we weren't sure. It wasn't until we asked Gladys that we discovered that is was the name of a card game – Auction 45s.

"Oh, you guys should come," she says to us. "It's lots of fun."

"Do you have to know how to play cards?" Pat asks. "I've only ever played Snap and Crazy 8s."

Gladys looks stunned. Obviously, she'd never met anyone with so little experience.

"Well, I play crib and stuff," I say, trying not to look too smug.

"Is that the one where you have to count to 15 on every hand?" asks Pat. "I tried that once, but they wouldn't let me use a calculator."

"Fifteen two, fifteen four, a pair is eight and one for His Nob is nine," I rhyme off glibly.

"Oh don't rub it in!" Pat grimaces.

"His Nob?" Gladys says.

"You know, the Jack."

"Oh, Nibs," says Gladys.

"How good do you have to be to play Auction 45s?" I ask. "Is it anything like Whist? Do you play in fours?"

"Well, yes...er, no. Oh, you'd pick it up real soon."

"If we come along to the Card Party, can you teach us?" asks Pat.

"Well, I'd better give you a couple of lessons first."

We say we'll think about it, especially since Pat is so obviously card-challenged.

"Are you ladies going to the Card Party?" asks Carl.

"Well, we thought we'd better take some lessons first," I say.

"Oh, you don't need to do that. You'd pick it up right quick. I've been playing ever since I was a little fellow and me grandfather taught me all he knew."

"Sounds like you're an expert," Pat says dubiously.

"Oh, I wouldn't say that. George, now, he's the expert. He pretty much takes them all on, chews them up, and spits them out. You don't dare make a mistake if you're playing with George. He never lets you forget it, neither."

"Sounds like a real gem of a gentleman. Will he be there?" I ask.

"Never misses a game," Carl assures me. "There's Uncle Billy and Bertha, Hilda and Mary, none of them ever misses a game. They're into cards real good. Probably enjoy some new blood," he finishes.

The blood analogy is too close to home for us. We decide to eschew Carl's game and George and company until we've had a few lessons from Gladys.

"They play something called tarabish up in Cape Breton," says Vera. "Some fellow brought it in from the Middle East, and now it's everywhere. They even have Tarabish Halls and games every night."

"Wow! Do you play?"

"Me? Are you crazy? I never learned how the thing went. I wouldn't dare put my nose into one of them games unless I knew what I was doing. They take their cards seriously in Cape Breton."

We decide this is true for the entire Maritimes. Cards parties are not for tyros. This is a professional sport.

"Let's go an ask Gladys to teach us," I say.

"No way! I'd sooner go bungee jumping or hang ten on some surf board than face George across a card table with only a few lessons from Gladys between me and total annihilation." Pat's face tells me she's not about to be persuaded otherwise.

"Probably just as well," Gladys consoles me. "You're a tad old to be learning all this new stuff, anyway."

> We all get heavier as we get older because there's a lot more information in our heads. – Vlade Divac, National Basketball Association player.

Instant Replay

The Card Party is the extreme sport for you if you:

1. Like to live on the edge.

2. Have friends visiting from away who think life in the Maritimes is dull.

3. Missed your bungee jumping appointment this week.

Degree Of Difficulty For This Sport

A piece of cake – laughable, really, a child under four years old could play this.

If I can do it, you can do it – a child over four years old could play this.

Anyone can do it – you have to pay attention some of the time.

Brain cells are used – you have to think some of the time.

☺☺   Don't try this at home – experienced sporters only.

How To Find This Sport

Ask the local family counsellor.